IMAGES
of America

BRIDGEVILLE

IMAGES
of America

BRIDGEVILLE

John F. Oyler
for the Bridgeville Area Historical Society

ARCADIA
PUBLISHING

Published by Arcadia Publishing
Charleston, South Carolina

Library of Congress Control Number: 2009930981

For all general information contact Arcadia Publishing at:
Telephone 843-853-2070
Fax 843-853-0044
E-mail sales@arcadiapublishing.com
For customer service and orders:
Toll-Free 1-888-313-2665

Visit us on the Internet at www.arcadiapublishing.com

*To the members of the Bridgeville Area Historical Society and their
dedication to the preservation of the history and heritage of the
Bridgeville area and to the Bridgeville historians who preceded us,
especially John Poellot, Daniel M. Bennett, and Jimmy Patton, who are
responsible for most of what we know about Bridgeville's early days.*

CONTENTS

ACKNOWLEDGMENTS

This book is a project of the Bridgeville Area Historical Society, and all images are from the society's collection. The society was organized in 2001 by members of a Bridgeville Community Association History Committee, established several years earlier in support of the community's centennial celebration. The society was founded to preserve the history and heritage of the Bridgeville community and the surrounding area. It has served as a repository for a large quantity of historical artifacts—photographs, newspaper articles, scrapbooks, etc.—in addition to providing 10 historical programs each year, many of which deal directly with the community.

Mary Weise was chairman of the original Bridgeville Community Association History Committee and has functioned as president of the Bridgeville Area Historical Society since its formation. The current board of directors consists of (chairman) Louis Colussy, Carole Bernabei, Lena Carrozza, Charles Degrosky, C. W. Hollenden, Florene Cherry Joyce, and Patte Winstein Kelley.

Other persons making significant contributions to the publication of this book include Diane Franjione, Ken Gastgeb, Midge Gilson, Russell Kovach, Marvin McCormick, Joseph Oyler, Kirsten Rogers, Alice Pesavento, Dana Spriggs, Dorothy Maioli Stenzel, and Don Toney. The coordinator of the compilation of material for the book is particularly indebted to his wife, Nancy L. Oyler, for her support.

INTRODUCTION

The village that eventually was incorporated as the Borough of Bridgeville in 1901 began as a small collection of houses and stores at the point where two primitive roads crossed Chartiers Creek. Prior to the arrival of European settlers following the French and Indian War, Native Americans followed Catfish Path paralleling Chartiers Creek from its headwaters near Washington, Pennsylvania, to the Ohio River. The early settlers improved the path and developed the Black Horse Trail along the same route. It was replaced by the first toll road in Western Pennsylvania, the Pittsburgh and Washington Pike, in the early 19th century. At the point where it crossed Chartiers Creek it also intersected a major east-west road, Noble's Trace. The Trace had been developed by Col. John Noble to provide an artery for wagon trains transporting cargo between his storehouse at Noblestown and eastern Pennsylvania communities.

The property at the crossing was owned by a Virginia planter, Thomas Ramsey. He improved the ford there and stationed an agent to collect tolls from the local farmers each time they used it. Passage of the Navigable Waters legislation in the early 1800s provided them with an opportunity to challenge his ownership of the ford. They filled a barge with grain at Canon's Mill (now Canonsburg) and successfully moved it down Chartiers Creek to the Ohio River. Having refuted Ramsey's ownership of the ford, the farmers then built a bridge across the creek, the bridge for which the village was eventually named.

By 1859, the village had become a collection of houses and stores serving a population of about 100 persons in addition to the farmers in the neighboring townships. The next few decades saw the development of numerous coal mines exploiting the Pittsburgh seam at the many places where it surfaced along Chartiers Creek. Initial mines were small operations, but they soon were supplanted by larger commercial facilities. The consequent influx of miners was felt by the community as it expanded accordingly. Many new stores and necessary services—medical, educational, and social—were established. New homes were constructed in every neighborhood.

By the end of the 19th century, Bridgeville had grown sufficiently to warrant independence from Upper St. Clair Township. A group of local business and professional men spearheaded a move for incorporation, which culminated in August 1901.

The new borough grew steadily in the next 50 years. Major industrial developments occurred in nearby portions of Collier and South Fayette Townships. The C. P. Mayer Brick Company, the Flannery Bolt Company, Universal Cyclops Steel, the Vanadium Corporation, the J. B. Higbee Glass Company, and the Selden Corporation were all established manufacturing facilities that provided employment for hundreds of local residents.

The industrial growth was matched by the development of a prosperous commercial district in Bridgeville. Banks, stores, a high school, hotels, movie theaters, and restaurants sprung up along Washington Avenue (a classic small town Main Street) and in several local neighborhoods. The commercial district included Baldwin Street, Railroad Street, Station Street, and Washington Avenue. Bridgeville became the prototypical small town, a local capitol of the neighboring townships. "Saturday night downtown" became a weekly event.

Bridgeville High School was the social center of the community. A concert or play at the high school would be attended enthusiastically by all the members of the community, regardless of their involvement with the school. Even more important were the school's sporting events, especially football and basketball. Three WPIAL (Western Pennsylvania Interscholastic Athletic League) football championships in the 1940s produced a maximum of community pride.

Sociological changes in the latter half of the 20th century dramatically changed Bridgeville. The major manufacturing businesses either failed or contracted significantly. The development of shopping malls in neighboring townships led to the demise of the major commercial enterprises in the downtown district. The school district merged with three other neighboring communities, and the high school moved out of Bridgeville.

As neighboring townships began to fill up with shopping malls and housing developments, Bridgeville's character gradually made the transition to a pleasant suburban residential community comparable to the ones evolving in all the neighboring townships. Today it is a fine place for middle class families to live and to enjoy the benefits of a traditional small town with an old-fashioned Main Street.

The history of any community is the cumulative history of the people who live in it. The first settlers in the Bridgeville area were farmers, mostly of English and Scotch-Irish descent, followed by tradesmen serving the farmers. In the late 1800s and early 1900s, immigrants from France, Germany, Italy, Slovenia, Lithuania, and other central European countries came to Bridgeville primarily to work in the coal mines. Sixteen Syrian families, mostly from the area around a small village named B'Soma, settled in Bridgeville in the 1920s, in the Baldwin Street neighborhood.

There have been African Americans in Bridgeville from its earliest days. The African American community grew in the early 1900s as families moved there to work in the mills. Their success in overcoming the obstacles of segregation paralleled the experience of other African American communities in the North.

Beginning in the 1930s, many third- and fourth-generation Americans moved to Bridgeville to take advantage of the easy transportation access into Pittsburgh, where they were able to find white-collar jobs. This trend has continued until the present. Each ethnic and social group has had a significant influence on the culture of the community. The resulting diversity has provided a rich environment for Bridgeville's residents.

This book has been organized chronologically, rather than by topic, with the objective of providing the reader with a general history of the evolution of the community from its earliest days as a frontier settlement through its development as an industrial/commercial center of the middle Chartiers Valley to its transition into a residential suburb of Pittsburgh, with a traditional small-town atmosphere. It is the objective of the Bridgeville Area Historical Society that this book motivates readers to enhance the body of historical information available by reporting errors and omissions to the society.

One

PRE-COLONIAL HISTORY

BEFORE 1770

Two events in geologic history greatly influenced the area that is now Western Pennsylvania. One hundred million years ago its portion of the North American Plate was located in a tropical environment, producing lush vegetation that became the raw materials for the coal beds deposited in the Carboniferous Age. Tectonic plate movement, uplifting, and erosion eventually produced the topography that we see today—a peneplain about 1,100 feet above sea level, with deep valleys cut by rivers and creeks. The most significant coal bed—the Pittsburgh seam—surfaces in many locations in the Chartiers Valley. This resource was the driving force for the massive industrial development in the Pittsburgh area in the second half of the 19th century, a development shared by Bridgeville.

The most recent Ice Age, beginning 100,000 years ago and ending 20,000 years ago, had no direct effect on the Chartiers Valley; the southern edge of the glaciers stopped about 50 miles north of Bridgeville. However, it did have a major influence on the watersheds of the major rivers in this area. Prior to the Ice Age, these rivers flowed north into a large inland sea where the Great Lakes are today. The glaciers and the debris they carried with them blocked this route and diverted the river system to the west, forming the present Ohio River and ensuring that Pittsburgh and Western Pennsylvania would eventually become the gateway to the West.

The first humans arrived in this area 15,000 years ago, primitive people who had crossed the Bering Land Bridge from Asia. Artifacts from their shelter at Meadowcroft, just a few miles south of Bridgeville, are among the earliest evidence of human habitation in the Western Hemisphere.

They were followed by a series of Native American societies, including the Monongahela people 1,000 years ago. Artifacts of their culture were uncovered in the 1920s when Gould City Hill was being developed and are valuable assets in the understanding of the Paleo-Indians.

By colonial times, this area was primarily a hunting ground for Native Americans, under the control of the Seneca tribe of the Six Nations. Delawares and Shawnees, displaced from their original homes by settlers, were the principal inhabitants. There were no permanent settlements in the Chartiers Valley, although a camp was maintained by a Delaware chief named Tingoocque (Catfish) beginning around 1765.

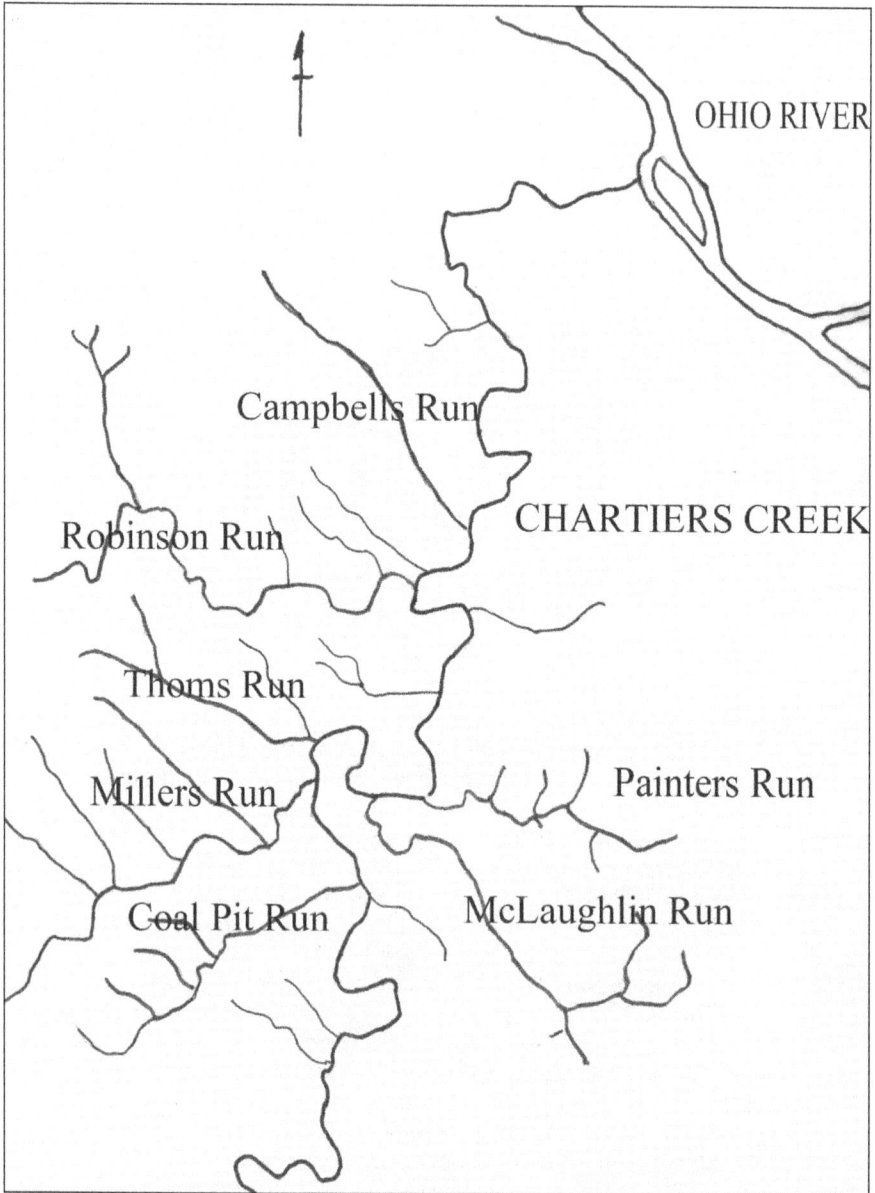

This map shows the Chartiers Creek watershed as it existed when the first settlers arrived. Chartiers Creek begins near Washington, Pennsylvania, and flows in a generally northerly direction through the current communities of Canonsburg, Bridgeville, Carnegie, Crafton, and McKees Rocks to its confluence with the Ohio River. South of Bridgeville the creek begins a meander to the north, then to the east, before returning again to the south. The Bridgeville community developed within the horseshoe loop of the meander, beginning where Coal Pit Run joins Chartiers Creek and ending at the point where McLaughlin Run enters Chartiers Creek. According to a popular legend, two brothers were going upstream on the creek searching for homesteads. One found a suitable site where today's Washington Avenue in Bridgeville crosses the creek at the north end of town. The other followed the creek 4 miles to find his own site. It turned out to be just three-quarters of a mile from his brother's claim, at the place where Washington Avenue crosses the creek at the south end of town.

Two

THE EARLY YEARS
1770–1876

The first Europeans to visit the Chartiers Valley were French soldiers occupying the forks of the Ohio and members of British armies sent to dislodge them during the French and Indian War. Christian Lesnett was a member of a Maryland company associated with Colonel Bouquet's expedition in 1763. In 1769, he returned, accompanied by two teenage sons, built a cabin, cleared some land, and planted rye, turnips, and corn. In the fall, he returned to Maryland, leaving his sons to protect his claim during the winter. He was delighted to find them alive and well when he returned in April 1770. Richard Boyce and his family settled in the Chartiers Valley in 1772; Nicholas Hickman and his family settled in 1774.

Prior to the arrival of the Europeans, a Native American trail called Catfish Path ran along the ridgetop paralleling the Chartiers Valley to the east. The settlers improved the trail and renamed it the Black Horse Trail. It crossed Chartiers Creek by a ford at the southern end of what is now Washington Avenue in Bridgeville. An east-west road, Noble's Trace, also crossed the creek at that point. Col. Henry Noble had established a trading post at what is now Noblestown and had cut a road through the wilderness to run pack trains to Carlisle. The storehouse he built near the ford was the first commercial building in the area.

Thomas Ramsey, owner of the land at the ford, decided to charge a toll for its use. The farmers resisted this action and had the creek declared a navigable stream by barging a cargo of grain from Canon's Mill (now Canonsburg) to the Ohio, negating Ramsey's claim to the ford. They then built a timber bridge that became a local landmark. "Meet you at the bridge" soon became "Meet you in Bridgeville." Between 1817 and 1834, the Washington Pike was built, following the alignment of the Black Horse Trail. A handful of houses and stores were constructed on the east side of the pike in Bridgeville; the Moses Middleswarth family occupied the west side. At the same time, the William Fryer family built a gristmill, school, and general store along McLaughlin Run.

Following Jonathan Middleswarth's death in 1868, the Middleswarth heirs subdivided the area west of the pike and opened it up for development residentially and commercially. The small community began to expand in both directions.

The original land claims are recorded in the 1914 Warrantee Atlas of Allegheny County. The area that is now Bridgeville is shown on the plate for Upper St. Clair Township. Thomas Ramsey originally owned most of the land west of Washington Avenue up to Station Street. Henry Evault owned land east of Washington Avenue and south of McLaughlin Run. Benjamin Rennoe's warrant included most of the land to the northeast. Moses Middleswarth and Moses Coulter acquired most of this land early in the 19th century: Middleswarth, west of Washington Avenue; Coulter, east.

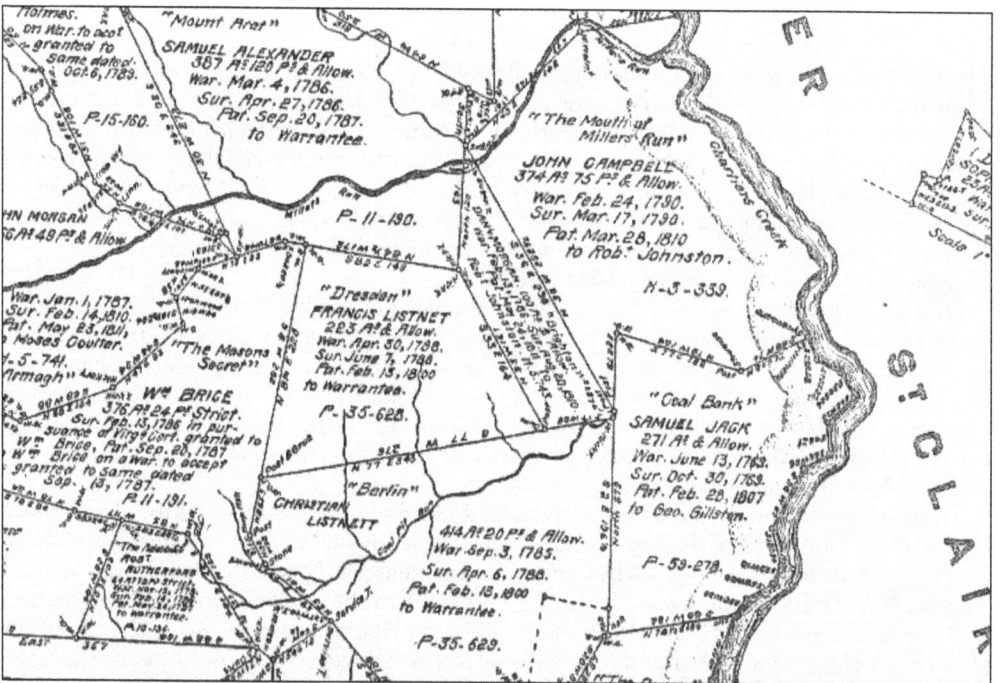

The warrants for the area that is now South Fayette Township, adjacent to Bridgeville, are shown on this map. Several of the warrantees are people whose history coincides with that of Bridgeville. Moses Middleswarth acquired much of the land east of Washington Avenue to supplement his holdings on the other side of Chartiers Creek. Christian Lesnett and his son Francis (shown as Listnt) were longtime residents of the region and significant citizens of the community. Neither John Campbell nor Samuel Jack appear in local historic annals; perhaps they were speculators who sold their claims and moved on.

12

The warrants for the portion of what is now Collier Township, adjacent to Bridgeville, are shown on this map. Col. John Neville and his son Presley Neville both settled in the Chartiers Valley after distinguished careers in the Revolutionary War. John Neville's plantation, Woodville, was the location of an early mansion built for Presley. It was directly across Chartiers Creek from John Neville's mansion, Bower Hill.

The warrants for the portion of what is now Scott Township, adjacent to Bridgeville, are shown on this map. The Neville holdings, the Avenue and Sidge Field, combined to comprise the portion of John Neville's plantation east of Chartiers Creek. This was the site of his mansion, Bower Hill, which was destroyed by fire in 1792 during the Whiskey Rebellion. William Fryer purchased this property in 1820. He and his son Samuel were early residents of Bridgeville.

Presley Neville's house, Woodville, survived the Whiskey Rebellion and was the residence for the Cowans (1815–1835) and the Wrenshalls (1835–1975). It has been lovingly restored and today is a National Historic Landmark, owned and maintained by Neville House Associates. Originally built in 1775, it was occupied by the Presley Neville family until 1814. The house is furnished in a manner consistent with the late 18th century.

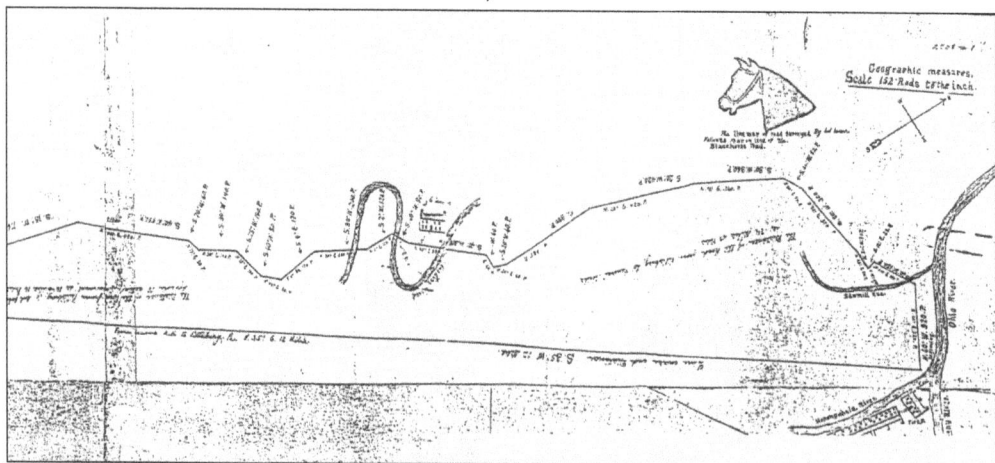

In pre-colonial times, a Native American trail, Catfish Path, led from Tingoocque's Camp near Washington, Pennsylvania, to the confluence of Saw Mill Run and the Ohio River. The settlers improved it and renamed it the Black Horse Trail. Part of it is shown on this survey. The trail crossed Chartiers Creek three times near Bridgeville and the Presley Neville House. The Pittsburgh and Washington Turnpike Company constructed a toll road along this route between 1817 and 1834. Today Interstate Highway I-79 follows the same general alignment from Washington, Pennsylvania, to Carnegie.

14

Originally built by Judge Henry Baldwin in the early 1800s and named Recreation, this house was acquired by Moses Coulter in 1812. It was located in Greenwood Place. Judge Baldwin was an influential citizen of Pittsburgh and Western Pennsylvania. His mansion in Meadville, now known as the Baldwin-Reynolds House, is maintained by the Crawford County Historical Society and is an excellent example of early-19th-century architecture.

Built by John McDowell around 1830, this house at 745 Washington Avenue was one of the first structures along the Washington Pike in Bridgeville. It was occupied by Dr. David Donaldson until his death in 1881. It was described in *Landmark Architecture of Allegheny County, Pennsylvania* as "a very agreeable example of the simple frame vernacular stemming from the late Classical style of the eighteenth century." It was razed in the 1990s to permit expansion of a funeral home.

This house, at 423 Washington Avenue, is the oldest remaining building in Bridgeville. It was built around 1830 and has been occupied continuously since then. Landmark Architecture of Allegheny County, Pennsylvania, described it as a "pleasant little vernacular Greek Revival brick house." It was a brick shop at one time and later an undertaker's establishment. The J. G. Murray family owned it in the late 1800s. It is currently occupied by Antiques on Washington.

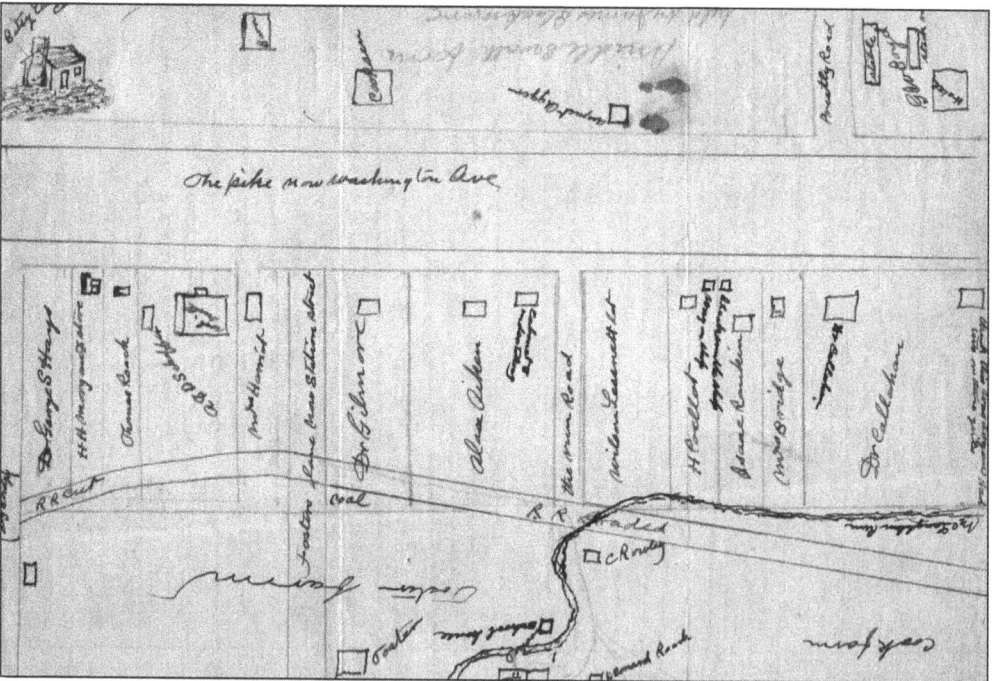

This map of Bridgeville in 1859 was drawn by John Poellot in the 1930s, in response to a request from his nephew Jimmy Patton, as to his recollection of the village when the Poellot family moved there from Sodom (now Clifton). In addition, he identified all of the families living in Bridgeville in 1859. The text of his description provides the introduction to chapter 3 on page 21.

Leonard and Eleanor Porter Fryer, originally from Ireland, settled on a farm near Bridgeville after he was wounded in the Indian wars in 1791. Their son William purchased the remnants of Gen. John Neville's plantation, Bower Hill, in 1820. He and his son William built a gristmill on McLaughlin Run near the intersection of McLaughlin Run Road and Baldwin Street and the Fryer School. Shown in this photograph is Bridgeville's first school when it opened in 1840. Retta Jones and Mary Reed were teachers at this school.

This photograph of the Poellot house at 353 Washington Avenue was taken in 1905, forty-six years after it was constructed. The Poellot family operated a wagon sales and repair business at that location. They later owned a hardware and feed store at 512 Washington Avenue, currently owned by the Sarasnick family.

The Schaffer woolen mill was a major industry in Bridgeville in the middle of the 19th century. Owned and operated by David and Andrew Schaffer, it converted raw wool into cloth, mostly for blankets and Linsey-Woolsy. Located on the southeast corner of the intersection of Washington Avenue and Station Street, it was destroyed by an explosion and fire in the 1870s. The artist responsible for this rendering is unknown.

This mansion, at 450 Washington Avenue, was built by Jonathan Middleswarth as a wedding gift to his fiancée. Unfortunately she changed her mind at the last minute and eloped with another man. He and his mother lived in the house alone until his death in 1868. It was a popular gathering place for the community for the rest of the century.

In celebration of the nation's centennial birthday, Allegheny County published a comprehensive atlas. Bridgeville was shown as part of the map for Upper St. Clair Township. The Chartiers Valley Railroad had just been completed. The small number of houses is consistent with the small population in the area at that time. McLaughlin Run is shown as Coal Run on this map. Similarly, Painter's Run is shown as Panther Run.

This map was an insert for the Upper St. Clair Township map in the 1876 Allegheny County Atlas. Nearly all of the community was on the east side of the Washington Pike. Shortly thereafter, the heirs of the Middleswarth family sold lots on the west side of the pike and Bridgeville expanded in that direction. The Norwood Hotel was under construction at the time and is not shown.

19

In 1876, Joseph Wright built the Norwood Hotel, a handsome Victorian showplace that attracted Pittsburgh residents as a summer resort. He and his wife, Mary, were ideal hosts for their guests. The grounds included an enclosed bowling alley, a path to Brady Spring high on the hill above Chartiers Creek, and a pavilion to house band concerts.

Horse-drawn wagons and buggies were the main method of transportation in Bridgeville in the 19th century. This photograph shows a fine team of horses responding to the commands of Harry Poellot. The Poellot family's wagon sales and repair business was one of Bridgeville's first industries.

Three

A TOWN IS BORN
1876–1901

Prior to the 1870s, the area that became Bridgeville was a handful of houses and shops, mostly on the east side of a country road—the Washington Pike. In the early 1930s, octogenarian John Powell described Bridgeville to his nephew Jimmy Patton as it was when his family moved there in 1859 as follows:

"The first structure on the west side of 'Washington Pike' after one crossed Chartiers Creek, heading south, was a hotel and stable run by Mr. and Mrs. G. W. Boyd. There also were five Boyd children. Across Prestley Road was the Middleswarth farm, at that time held by James Blackamore. The Agger family, including two children, occupied the house just north of [today's] Murray Street. The next house was occupied by the Cook sons; it was close to the site of the PNC Bank today. Farther south was the 'Easton Cabin,' which housed five Eastons.

"Directly across the 'Pike,' on the east side, was the residence of Dr. and Mrs. Hayes and their five children. Next, moving north along the 'Pike,' was the store of H. H. Morgan. The Morgan family included seven children, at that time. Thomas Roach occupied the next house with Mrs. Phillips and four younger Roaches. The next establishment was a wool mill owned and operated by Mr. and Mrs. Schaeffer and five offspring.

"On the southeast corner of Foster's Lane [now Station street] and the 'Pike' was the home of Mrs. Harriot and her son. Across Foster's Lane was the property of Dr. and Mrs. Gilmore. Then came the home of Mr. and Mrs. Alan Aiken, and four children. Adjacent to it was a building identified as cabin making and undertaking. Apparently the cabinetmaker also made coffins.

"Wilson Lesnett owned the property just north on 'the run road;' next door were the Poellots, including three sons. Next came a blacksmith shop, followed by the home of Mr. and Mrs. Isaac Rankin and their three daughters. The next home housed four ladies named Bridge. Directly opposite Prestley Road was the home of Dr. and Mrs. Calahan and their five children. The Logan family lived in the last house south of Chartiers Creek."

The next decade brought numerous changes, producing a classic American small town—the construction of the Chartiers Valley Railroad, the establishment of the Norwood Hotel, and the opening of the coal mines.

In 1886, the Bridgeville School was located at the corner of Locust and Hickman Streets. J. G. Murray (1) and Dr. W. Gilmore (2) were directors. Josie (Reed) Couch (3) was the teacher. The lot on which the school was located was purchased by Henry Poellot from the Middleswarth heirs. The building was sold to the Upper St. Clair School District when the school was established. It was later owned by Macedonia Maioli.

Located at the intersection of Murray Avenue and Washington Avenue, Billy Winstein's store in Murray Hall was a popular gathering place in 1888. In front of the store are, from left to right, Ed Roach, Dr. David Gilmore, Charlie Couch, W. J. (Billy) Winstein, Andy Rankin, Reuben Pugh, Ulysses Ferree, an unidentified child, and an unidentified man.

Bridgeville Pa. Photograph Taken Feb. 1887

This 1887 photograph of Bridgeville provides a view southeast along Station Street. The railroad station, Sam Foster's store, and the Norwood Hotel are prominent. It was the basis for a well-known painting by David Rankin. It is the earliest photograph showing key structures in the community.

David Rankin painted this picture based on the photograph at the top of this page. It is an excellent portrayal of a classic American small town in the midst of a 19th-century winter.

"Carpets, Bedsprings, & Bedding" could be bought at an affordable price at Amos Fryer's furniture store on McLaughlin Run Road in the 1870s. It also served as the first home for Fryer's undertaking business, an enterprise that began in 1875. Fryer later built a commercial building on the southeast corner of Washington Avenue and Station Streets, which was sold to C. P. Mayer in the 1890s.

The Otterman Manufacturing Company had a busy operation on Washington Avenue in the 1890s. This photograph shows the blacksmith/forge shop and a group of workers. The emphasis on hardware to serve the horse-and-buggy trade is apparent.

Bridgeville Station
1891

In 1871, the Chartiers Valley Railroad was completed and put into operation. It linked Bridgeville to Canonsburg and Washington to the south and to Carnegie and Pittsburgh to the north. Easy access into the city dramatically increased its importance to Bridgeville residents. This 1891 photograph shows the Chartiers Valley Railroad station with Sam Foster's store on Station Street behind it.

The first school building at 431 Washington Avenue was this two-story frame structure with a central bell tower. It was built in 1893 and replaced by a brownstone building of nearly similar size and design in 1905. This school replaced the Locust Street school.

The first class of students to graduate from Washington School included, from left to right, Mary Melvin, Grace (Shaw) Lesnett, Mary Jones, Leith Baird, Edna Fryer, and A. M. Kelley. They graduated in 1893, having completed 11 years of elementary and secondary education.

The Poellot family established a hardware store at 512 Washington Avenue and operated it until 1934, when it was sold to the Sarasnick family. It is still in operation and is well known as the place to look for hardware that cannot be found anywhere else. Will Poellot (left) and George Washington Poellot are shown in front of the store.

Florian Kopach and his wife, Mary (Czonc), came to America from Slovenia to find a better life. Kopach was a coal miner for most of his life. They are shown in this family portrait with their children, from left to right, Rudolf, Frank, Mary, and Fred. Because the photographer was late arriving, Kopach had to change into his work clothes. The resulting picture emphasized the importance of his work to the maintenance of a good life for his family.

This photograph presents a view south on Washington Avenue in the mid-1890s. The building at the left was purchased by C. P. Mayer from Amos Fryer in 1892. The Mayer family lived on the second floor of the Mayer Building. Wagner's general store on the opposite side of the street also offered "quality loans."

An unidentified family posed for this fetching portrait in front of their Victorian home in the 1890s.

The Pennsylvania Railroad Station is shown in this 1897 photograph. Foster's store and the Norwood Hotel are in the background. The railroad provided easy access into Pittsburgh with seven trains running each way daily. It became practical for businessmen working in the city to commute each day, maintaining their homes in Bridgeville.

John F. Hosack was a prominent merchant in Bridgeville in the 1890s. This photograph shows his store and one of his wagons used for general hauling. Hosack ran for office as a Republican in Bridgeville's first election and was elected burgess.

Martial music was all the rage in 1898. This band, none of whose members are identified, consisted mostly of horns, plus a couple of drums.

The Webb Murray family built this house at 432 Washington Avenue in the mid-1890s. Identified in this 1898 photograph are Mrs. Webb Murray, Mrs. A. B. Murray holding Alberta Murray, and Jim and Sara Murray. The cyclist is not identified. By the 1950s, the building served as the Lavelle Funeral Home.

A group of amateur thespians posed for this picture in the Bethany Church sanctuary on April 14, 1898. They are, from left to right, (first row) Ed Foster, Ella Baird, Lib Vance, Lou Hosack, Minnie Hopper, Billy Winstein, Joe Alexander, and Howard Morrison; (second row) Charlie Morgan, Lizzie McMillen, Carl Roach, Lew Wallace, Sadie Calamus, Margaret Poellot, Lou Patton, Mary Connor, Jennie Russell, Nellie Poellot, Louise Richey, George Alexander, Sue Morrison, Elizabeth Weaver, and John Vance; (third row) Sam Patton, Sherman McMillen, Harry Couch, Wash Poellot, Capitola Donaldson, Linn Hanna, Bob Cook, and Frank Russell. The play was titled *The District School at Blueberry Corners*.

Amateur theatrics brought a taste of culture to Bridgeville in its early years. This group of dramatists performed a play called *Old Country School*. The cast included Harry Couch, George Alexander, Capitola Donaldson, Elizabeth Weaver, Mrs. Lou Patton, Washington Poellot, Lizzie McMillen, Mrs. Washington Poellot, Louise Lyon, and Sue Lowry.

Built in 1893, the S. W. Patton family house is shown around 1900 with members of the family on the front porch and in the yard. The house was located at 701 Bank Street, on the corner of Bank Street and Gregg Avenue. At the top of the hill, Bank Street eventually became Mayview Road, an important link to the state hospital at Mayview.

Originally built by Judge Henry Baldwin in the early 1800s and named Recreation, this house was acquired, successively, by Moses Coulter in 1812, by Walter Foster in 1844, and by David Gilmore in 1879. Gilmore's daughter Capitola Donaldson inherited it. The Donaldson family occupied it until 1948. It was located in Greenwood Place.

William Warrensford lived in this cabin, across Chartiers Creek from Bethany Church, in the early 1900s. He was a cabinetmaker and carpenter who came to the Bridgeville area in 1850. He and his wife, Jane (Stone), had nine children; their descendants were prominent citizens of the community. Thomas Warrensford built Dr. Fife's home, the Samuel Foster residence, and the third floor of Washington School.

The 1901 Bridgeville Baseball Club was represented by the players in this photograph. They are, from left to right, (first row) Max Kinney, P. Quiqley, Charles Kinney, William Goehring, and Charles Mayer; (second row) Frank Mayer, M. R. Mallery, William Humphries, and William McCaffrey; (third row) Charles Sims, David M. Bennett, R. Marshman, and William Woodall. Mallery was the manager, and Bennett was the captain.

M.R. Mallery "Manager"   D.M. Bennett "Captain"

Season 1901

left to right
First Row M,Kinney. P Quigley C.Kinney.Goehring ,C.Mayer
Second "   F.Mayer M Mallery ,Humphries,McCaffrey,
Third "   Sims   Bennet, Marshman, Woodall

Albert B. Murray purchased the mansion Jonathan Middleswarth had built at 430 Washington Avenue in 1901. He is shown with his children, Sara (Froelick), Jim, Alberta (Baker), Anna (Metz), and Mary (Fitzsimmons) and his wife, Lizzie Wiley Murray.

Because the Pittsburgh Coal Seam was located at about the same elevation as Chartiers Creek in the Bridgeville area, it was easy to locate good sources of coal and to mine directly into the hillsides. The area quickly became a center of bituminous coal mining. These five men were pictured around 1900 on their way to work in one of the mines.

By the beginning of the 20th century, mechanized coal cars had replaced mules in the mine shafts. Miners and the coal that they dug were transported from the underground seams to the surface and the coal tipples by cars like these shown here.

Four

INCORPORATION
1901–1910

By 1900, it was obvious that Upper St. Clair Township could not adequately provide infrastructure for the growing community. A group of 94 property owners representing the 2,400 residents of Bridgeville petitioned the Court of Quarter Sessions of Allegheny County for permission to secede from Upper St. Clair and be incorporated as a borough.

Attorney George P. Murray, John F. Hosack, J. D. Meise, W. W. Murray, George S. Orth, and W. G. Pugh presented the petition on March 11, 1901. On July 27, 1901, the court entered an order decreeing incorporation of Bridgeville as a borough. Hosack was elected burgess; Dr. S. J. S. Fife, president of borough council; S. A. Foster, treasurer; John F. Vance, clerk; and Robert L. McMillen, constable.

The next decade saw continued growth. C. P. Mayer established the Bridgeville Land Improvement Company to develop property in Collier Township just north of Bridgeville. The C. P. Mayer Brick Company was the first tenant in 1903. The Flannery brothers established the Flannery Bolt Company there in 1904 and the American Vanadium Corporation in 1907. Higbee Glass built its plant there in 1907. The Universal Rolling Mill Company completed the development when its new plant was constructed in 1909.

In the early 1900s, George Gould attempted to expand his Wabash Railway system into a transcontinental route. A key component of this was a link into downtown Pittsburgh. This link was constructed in 1903, giving Bridgeville additional access into the city. Although the Gould ambitions were never completely realized, the railroad through Bridgeville has survived and today is part of the Norfolk Southern system.

The frame school building at 431 Washington Avenue was replaced by a brownstone building in 1904. St. Agatha's Roman Catholic congregation built its first church on Station Street. Small family-owned stores were opened in many neighborhoods, especially along Baldwin and Railroad Streets. The popularity of automobiles generated new businesses selling, repairing, and providing gasoline for them.

This 1903 photograph shows "Kid" Myers being called out trying to steal home. Ironically, Myers spent most of his life as a member of the Bridgeville police force, including many years as police chief. Baseball was a popular sport for young adult men at the turn of the 20th century.

Early in the 20th century, George Gould attempted to put together a collection of railroads, the Wabash System, providing transcontinental passenger service. In 1903, he acquired land in Bridgeville and announced plans for construction of a massive railroad facility and a new community, Gould City. This brochure was published to encourage investors to travel to Bridgeville and evaluate the opportunity. Although the railroad was built, the Bridgeville facilities did not materialize. The principal memory of Gould is the perpetuation of his name on Gould City Hill.

Dr. Quentin S. Kocher owned one of the first automobiles in Bridgeville. He is shown in this photograph with two children and a dog. Note that the steering wheel is on the right side of the front seat.

This view of Washington Avenue in the early 1900s provides a vivid contrast between the primitive vehicles on the street and the modern Bridgeville Trust Company Building, opened in 1902. A poolroom, a bargain store, and James Filento's grocery store are in the left part of the photograph.

When the new Bridgeville Trust Company building was constructed on the northwest corner of the intersection of Washington Avenue and Station Street, Daniel M. Bennett's Drugstore occupied half of the first floor. Bennett learned the pharmacy business in Patterson's Drugstore, beginning in 1896. He eventually acquired the business and operated it initially in the Bridgeville Trust Company Building and later in a separate building at 444 Washington Avenue.

The Flannery brothers, Joseph and James, were the first clients for C. P. Mayer's Bridgeville Land Improvement Company when they built the Flannery Bolt Company plant in 1904 to produce locomotive stay bolts. During World War II, the plant produced machine gun barrels.

The crossing guard at the Station Street crossing had a responsible job with many trains passing through each day. This photograph, taken in the early 1900s, also shows the southbound freight platform. Note the billboard in the background advertising J. H. Rankin's store.

When this photograph of Bridgeville's Lower End was taken around 1905, the Bridgeville Hotel was owned and operated by Matt Mallery. Angelo Pepe came to Bridgeville in 1901 and worked at the hotel for Mallery. In 1913, Pepe and his wife, Lucy (Carrozza), purchased the hotel from Mallery. The steeple of Zion Lutheran Church can be seen at the left side of the photograph as well as homes on St. Clair Street and Prestley Road.

This photograph shows the Samuel A. Foster residence, 527 Station Street, in the early 1900s. The Foster family operated a busy grocery store at the corner of Station and Railroad Streets. At one time, the Bridgeville Post Office was operated within Foster's store; Sam Foster was postmaster.

This photograph shows a happy group of young people in A. B. Murrays' backyard in 1906. Recreation was much simpler in those days but just as satisfying as the more sophisticated activities that succeeded it.

Albert Murray and his family are shown in this 1906 photograph enjoying the ambiance of their backyard. Family life was important to everyone—enjoyed by the affluent as well as by those less fortunate.

Four fashionable young ladies posed for this photograph in A. B. Murray's side yard in 1906. Photography was a popular activity in the early 1900s, with many of the photographs being printed as postcards.

It was feeding time for A. B. Murray's dog when this 1906 photograph was taken. The participants include, from left to right, an unidentified woman, Sarah Murray, Lizzie Murray, Alberta Murray, an unidentified woman, Anna Murray, and Albert Murray.

The interior of the A. B. Murray home was typical of houses of the period. This 1906 photograph shows a bedroom in the mansion. Note the profusion of photographs on the dresser and on the wall, the gaudy large-patterned wallpaper, and the incised decoration on the dresser.

J. B. Higbee Glass Factory, Bridgeville, Pa.

The J. B. Higbee Glass Company built a plant in Bridgeville in 1907 to produce a popular line of tableware. The plant was sold to General Electric in 1918. It continues to produce industrial glass products in this plant today. Higbee glassware, distinguished by its bumblebee trademark, is still a popular collector's item.

From left to right, Callie and Maggie Morgan and their parrot are shown in front of their home at 537 Station Street in 1907. The parrot's name has been lost to posterity. This photograph is especially descriptive of life in a typical American small town a century ago.

44

By 1907, Bridgeville had expanded to the east as far as Elm Street. This photograph shows the intersection of Bank Street and Gregg Avenue. The Patton home is at the left and the Frank Mayer home at the right. The area known as Bank Property was bounded by Gregg Avenue, Chartiers Street, Elm Street, and Bank Street. The area had been developed by Peoples Savings Bank.

In the early part of the 20th century, the Ladies Fancy Work group was a popular women's social organization. This 1908 photograph includes, from left to right, (first row) Mrs. Landgraf, Louise Lyon Richey, Mrs. G. P. Murray, and Mrs. G. W. Poellot; (second row) Mrs. Flagg, Mrs. Hosack, Jane Gilmore, Mrs. A. B. Murray, Mrs. Cook, and Mrs. S. G. Lyon; (third row) Mrs. Mealy, Mrs. Wilcox, Mrs. J. F. Murray, and Mrs. Shidle.

Bridgeville's first "auto livery" at 438 Washington Avenue provided taxi and bus service between Bridgeville and Cecil, as well as transfer and moving services. Started by Joseph Supan, it developed into a significant bus company after World War I. Joann's Beauty Shop now occupies the building.

Macedonia Maioli and his wife, Zelinda (Verzellesi), came to Bridgeville from Guastalla, Italy, in 1888, eventually moving to 226 Hickman Street. Maioli originally worked in the coal mines and as a stone mason at Mayview. His wife tended a grocery store. He later had a wholesale liquor business and kept a stable of racehorses in a barn on Hickman Street.

The Maioli children were orphaned when both parents, mother in 1910 and father in 1911, died. They moved into a house at 409 Washington Avenue. Shown in this photograph are, from left to right, (first row) Arthur, Raymond, and George; (second row) Anita (O'Neil) and Sarah (Silhol); (third row) Mary (Altimoni), John, and Natalie (Fagan). Another son, Edward, died as an infant in 1906.

The Edmund Robert Weise family came to Bridgeville in 1913. They originally came to Western Pennsylvania from Germany in 1881. This family photograph, taken around 1909, includes everyone except Marie, who had not yet been born. From left to right, they are (first row) Karl and Elnora (Rankin); (second row) Paul, Edmund, Alma Georgi (holding Ralph), and Clara (Jones); (third row) Louis, Minnie (Stenzel), and Frank.

This *c.* 1909 photograph shows the John C. Crum family in front of their home at 711 Chartiers Street. Crum was the son of David Wilson Crum and Margaret Frye Crum, who came to Bridgeville in 1870. The team of oxen on the cover of this book belonged to John Crum. The house is now owned by Terry Wright.

William Frank Russell and his wife, Jennie (Galbraith), moved to Bridgeville in 1890, where he functioned as station agent for the Pennsylvania Railroad. He later operated a livery stable, undertaking business, and Nickelodeon at 336 Station Street. This 1909 photograph shows two of the Russell family's hearses. The white hearse was used for children and the black one for adults. The building was later occupied by E. A. Motor Company.

Joseph and James Flannery founded the American Vanadium Corporation in 1907 and built a plant to produce ferrovanadium, an important alloying agent in high-strength steel. They became aware of the importance of vanadium as an alloying agent while they were researching materials for use in the products of their Flannery Bolt Company.

This photograph shows Bower Hill Road crossing the Pennsylvania Railroad with Cook's Hill in the background in the early 1900s. Bluff Street is winding up and crossing over the top of Cook's Hill. Many new homes had recently been built on Liberty and Union Streets. The original Pennsylvania Railroad Freight Station is in the center of the photograph.

Five

MELTING POT
1911–1920

The second decade of the 20th century found Bridgeville continuing to grow. In later years, its residents marveled at the ethnic diversity of the community and its role as a melting pot. The original inhabitants were primarily of English and Scotch-Irish stock. As the borough grew, immigrants from many other nations arrived and contributed to its rich, multicultural environment.

Original homelands of these people included Germany, Italy, Austria-Hungary, Poland, Slovenia, Lithuania, and Syria. There were African Americans in Bridgeville from the earliest days; John Poellot's informal 1859 census included the Easton family. Each ethnic group strove to achieve integration into the American culture without losing the treasured aspects of the culture it had left behind.

Sometimes this was characterized by the formation of ethnically based churches. The German community founded Zion Lutheran Church and continued services in German into the 1940s. The Syrian community founded St. George's Orthodox Church; the African Americans, the First Baptist Church; and the Lithuanians, St. Anthony's Roman Catholic Church.

Another way to retain cultural characteristics was the formation of ethnically based social and fraternal organizations. The Bridgeville Italian Club was founded as the Italian Mutual Beneficial Society in 1910. Two Slovenian clubs were formed: the Slovenian Mutual Beneficial Aid Society at 202 Liberty Street and S. N. P. J. Lodge No. 295 on Ridge Road. People of German descent formed the Dutch Club at 929 McLaughlin Run Road; it was renamed the American Independent Beneficial Society at the beginning of World War II.

World War I had a heavy impact on Bridgeville, with many young men serving their country and with seven making the ultimate sacrifice. The influenza epidemic at the end of World War I was also severe. Fryer's Funeral Home buried 121 victims of the epidemic, including its director, Samuel Blake Fryer.

John Zadro came from Italy in 1901 to Bridgeville, where he met and married Gemma Bigi. In 1912, they built this house at 627 Baldwin Street and established the Zadro Bottling Works and later the Zadro Distributing Company. It is interesting to see the horses and the outhouse in the backyard and the laundry hanging out to dry behind the house on Cook's Hill, across McLaughlin Run.

The Wallace Building at 533 Washington Avenue showed evidence of prosperity in this 1911 photograph. It was destroyed by fire in the 1990s. The contrast between the modern appearance of the building and the horse and buggy in front of it is striking.

This photograph is the left half of a pair taken from Gould City Hill in 1911, looking east. Ramsey Avenue is the street in the right foreground, with Chess Street extending to the left. The Wabash Railroad is just beyond Ramsey Avenue. Its passenger station can be seen at the Murray Avenue crossing. Washington Avenue, where Washington School is prominently located, crosses the middle of the photograph. The Bank Property development can be seen in the distance.

This photograph is the right half of the pair taken from Gould City Hill in 1911. Ramsey Avenue is in the foreground with the Wabash Railroad beyond it. Station Street runs diagonally from left to right across the photograph. The First Methodist Church can be seen at the intersection of Chess Street and Station Street. The steeple of Bethany Church is prominent in the background, with the Chartiers Creek valley beyond it.

Old Donaldson House
745 Washington ave.   1911-12

In 1911, Washington Avenue had not yet been paved. The white building in the middle of the photograph is the old Donaldson House at 745 Washington Avenue. Note that the cars have steering wheels on the right side and that they are driving on the left side of the street.

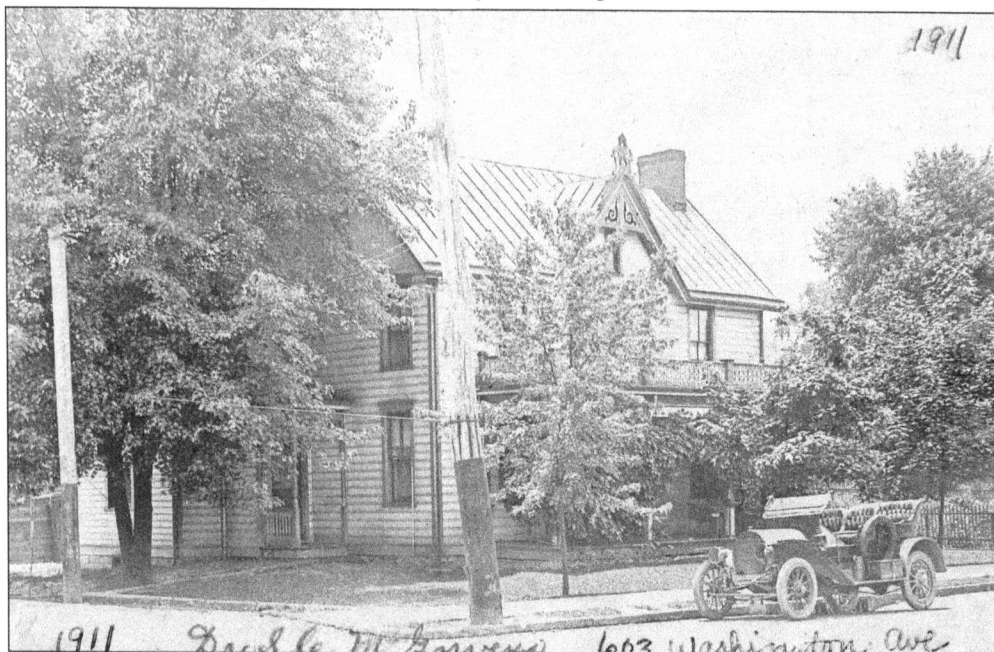

1911   1911   Dr. S. G. McGarvey   603 Washington ave.

Dr. Samuel. G. McGarvey and his new bride, Mary (Stamm), came to Bridgeville in 1901 after his graduation from medical school. Their home and his office were at 603 Washington Avenue in 1911. He practiced medicine at that location until his death in 1951, when his son Dr. Myron McGarvey succeeded him. In addition to his private practice, Dr. McGarvey's industrial practice included nearby coal mines and manufacturing companies.

Gregg Avenue was the first street developed in Bank Property. By 1911, it sported wooden sidewalks and telephone poles, although it had not yet been paved. The houses in this photograph, from right to left, were occupied by the Poellot family, the Franks family, the Meise family, and the Orth family.

Elm Street was the eastern border of Bridgeville in 1911; the Foster family owned this fine home on Elm Street. The alley beyond Elm Street was the boundary to the East of Bank Property. The homes on Elm Street have been well maintained and are the basis for an attractive neighborhood today.

Although the Norwood Hotel had begun to lose some of its summer resort business by 1911, it still was a popular gathering place for Bridgeville residents, some of whom were enjoying libations in its bar. The bar is gaily decorated for the Christmas holidays. The December 1911 calendar on the wall is from G. Freucht and Sons, Carnegie. Mr. and Mrs. George Ritter had purchased the hotel from the Wright family in 1900.

By 1912, the school at 431 Washington Avenue had been modified by the addition of a third floor. It housed all 11 grades at that time and was a major cultural/social asset for the community. After Lincoln School (on Gregg Avenue) was built in 1924, Washington School functioned as a grade school until it was destroyed by fire in 1958.

In 1912, the Bridgeville Post Office was located on Station Street. RFD mail delivery was accomplished by horse and buggy. Web Connor, directly behind the buggy, was postmaster and also handled RFD Route No. 1. Paul Tidball, who had RFD Route No. 2, is behind the horse. This building served as post office until the new one was built at the corner of Washington Avenue and Hickman Street.

Postal service involved much more than the delivering and picking up of mail. This photograph shows a group of postal workers busy sorting and distributing mail, as well as waiting on customers at the window.

The Italian Mutual Beneficial Society of Bridgeville was organized early in the 20th century, largely through the efforts of Frank Truzzi. After meeting in private homes, the Court of Allegheny County granted the society a charter. They then met in Dominic Collavo's building on Baldwin Street until 1922, when they moved into new quarters at 414 Margaret Street.

The interior of the Italian club featured an elegant dining room and bar, complete with spittoons. The club boasted 125 members by 1921 and was a hotbed for bocce (Italian lawn bowling). In addition to serving the male portion of the Italian American community, in 1948, the Italian Sisters of Bridgeville was formed, with Alice Pesavento as president.

James Franks, standing at right, was the stationmaster at the Pennsylvania Railroad Station in the early 1900s. One evening in 1915, he was killed attempting to thwart a robbery of the office there. His murderers were never apprehended, although several individuals were considered suspects 20 years later.

Four Civil War veterans posed in front of a brand new 48-star flag around 1912. They are, from left to right, Andy Rankin, David Bowers, John Warrensford, and David Crum.

On May 14, 1914, Bethany Presbyterian Church celebrated the centennial of its incorporation. In 1814, the church was located along what is now the Sygan-Presto Road. The congregation established a mission in Bridgeville in the 1860s and in 1889 built their church at 740 Washington Road.

The Stephen Kovach family is shown in this 1915 photograph. They are, from left to right, (first row) Caroline, Stephen Jr., and Albert; (second row) Grizella, Stephen G. Kovach Sr., Katharine Yeager Kovach, Charles, and Leona; (third row) Frank, Clara, Elizabeth, and Minnie. The inset is a photograph of Florence, who was born in 1917.

The Leon Volle family emigrated from the Ardèche region of France in 1907 to seek a better life in America. They initially settled in Morgan. Leon had to move his family from Morgan because of his union activities at the mine, so he bought a house at 724 Chess Street. Shown in this 1915 photograph are, from left to right, Louis Julien Volle, Leon Jacques Louis Volle Sr., Leon Jacques Louis Volle Jr., Leona Marie Volle (D'Andrea), Maria Philomine Teyssier (Volle), Leon Fialon (a nephew), and Mary Leonine Volle (Mouret).

This photograph of the Bethany Presbyterian Church in 1915 is of the second building to be constructed at this site. The original structure, a frame building called the "Lord's Barn," was constructed in 1870. It was replaced by this building with its distinctive steeple in 1889. The church has continued to prosper and grow and currently serves a large congregation in the surrounding area.

This photograph shows the Wagner family set for a ride around 1915. In the front seat are, from left to right, Valentine Wagner and his daughter Marcella (later Munnell). In the second seat are sons George, Ralph, and Charles. In the backseat are son Valentine Wagner Jr. and Mrs. Wagner.

This c. 1915 photograph records a Memorial Day parade. The parade has progressed from Washington Avenue across the south bridge and is well up the Washington Pike, en route to Melrose Cemetery.

The caption for this photograph reads, "This is the hungry bunch that comes up at Noon (from Russell's to 701 and 707 Bank Street) and that is just the way they look." Pictured are, from left to right (in the car) Leslie Patton, Frank Russell, Walter Patton, Bill Russell, Bert Russell, and Martie Russell; (standing) Philip Green, W. F. Russell, Myrtle Russell, Margaret Vance, Jennie Russell, Isabelle Russell, and Elizabeth Vance.

These two buildings were in the 300 block on the west side of Washington Avenue. The house at the left was the homestead of the Behling family. The building beyond it was the residence of the Omera Panizza family and the location of their grocery store. It later was also the site of the Bridgeville Bottling Works, a producer of Indian Springs soft drinks.

Shown here are members of the Bridgeville High School classes of 1916 and 1918. There was no graduating class in 1917, as the school went from three years of high school to four that year. Some of the students are identified, from left to right, (first row) T. Walter Jones (1), Joseph Lutz (5), and Lawrence Rankin (6); (second row) Eleanor Browner (2), Margaret Harmuth (3), Mary (Clark) Hartman (4), Clara (Jones) Weise (5), Marion (McCracken) Freed (8), and Louella (Pierce) Martin (9); (third row) Della Warensford (2), Bernadine McCaffrey Conroy (7), Lois Gallagher (9), and teacher Joseph Ferree (11); (fourth row) Elmer Collavo (6).

Seven Bridgeville residents, including Rudolph Kovach who is pictured, lost their lives during World War I. The other young men were Albert Comstock, Roy Purnell, Ivor Reese, Raymond Roach, Adam Spohn, and Lloyd Warensford. Purnell's story is especially poignant. After the war, the U.S. government made it possible for war widows to go to France to visit the graves of their deceased, but because she was African American, Viola Purnell was denied this opportunity. Her employer, Dr. Fife, provided the necessary funds to allow her to make the trip.

Six

PROSPERITY
1921–1930

Following the end of World War I and the influenza epidemic, Bridgeville settled down for an era of prosperity—the Roaring Twenties. The returning veterans were welcomed home and quickly became the focus of activities honoring them for their service. The population continued to grow, and many new homes were built and new businesses established.

In 1919, C. P. Mayer had caught the aviation bug and established the first airport in Western Pennsylvania, Mayer Field—the headquarters of the Mayer Aircraft Company. The airfield saw a succession of new aircraft models, including the *Pride of Pittsburgh*, a Ryan B-1 Brougham that was a sister ship to Lindbergh's *Spirit of St. Louis*. Mayer Aircraft became the local sales agent for a number of different aircraft companies.

The initiation of Bigi Bus service initially to Dormont and eventually into Pittsburgh provided additional effective access into the city for commuters working downtown as well as for shoppers. A trip into the city to visit the department stores and the five-and-dime stores was a popular event.

In the mid-1920s, a new school building was constructed on Gregg Avenue to house junior high and high school students. The first high school class to graduate from it was the class of 1926. Washington School was relegated to an elementary school for the first six grades. The increased population provided enough students to fill both schools. The entire community welcomed the construction of the school and the increased opportunities for cultural and athletic activities that it provided.

Burkey Jones represented Bridgeville as a member of the 1924 U.S. Olympic Soccer Team. A swimming pool was constructed and quickly became a popular spot in the summer. A world-class automobile-racing complex attracted competitors from across the country.

Joseph Supan and several of his brothers operated a small bus and taxi business, up Miller's Run, connecting Bridgeville and Cecil in the early 1920s. The operation was sold to Penn Bus Lines in 1928 and eventually became part of the community transit system. Supan later acquired a franchise from John Collavo that became the Oriole Bus Line.

This wrought iron through truss bridge carried the Washington Pike across Chartiers Creek at the south end of Bridgeville. A similar bridge performed the same function at the north end of the community. Both bridges were replaced with steel pony trusses in 1929.

The mansion at 430 Washington Avenue, shown in this 1920 photograph, was occupied by the Murray family until 1929, when it was acquired by Dr. Quentin S. Kocher. It eventually was razed to permit construction of a parking lot.

The Delphus Theater, at 429 Railroad Street, was a popular destination for moviegoers in the days before "talking pictures." This *c.* 1922 photograph shows an eager crowd ready to watch silent screen actor Eddie Polo in the fourth episode of *Do or Die*, titled "Hidden Danger."

In addition to providing frequent passenger service from Bridgeville into Pittsburgh, the Pennsylvania Railroad was an important freight link to the rest of the country. This photograph shows 2 trunks, 14 packing cases, and 2 wagons filled with barrels ready to be shipped out.

When Angelo and Lucy Pepe operated the Bridgeville Hotel at 112 Washington Avenue, it was a popular semipermanent residence for families of men working at the mills—Universal, Vanadium, or General Electric. These people had regular tables for meals. In this c. 1922 photograph, the signs advertise "Liquors and Beer," "Sandwiches," "Dance," "Turtle Soup," and "Ravioli."

In the photograph, the following labels appear: Friers Hill, McLaughlin Run Road, Bank St., Chartiers St, Chartiers Creek, P.CC.& St.L. RR, Mill St→, McLaughlin Run Road↗, Baldwin So, all Road St, C.C.& St.L. RR, shington Ave., View of, Station St), Be-M branch, Hickman St., Bridgeville From the Clouds. Taken By Jas. Wagner C.P. Mayer Air Field July 1922.

In July 1922, James Wagner took this aerial photograph of Bridgeville from an airplane from Mayer Field. It was given the title "Bridgeville from the clouds." Main streets are identified as well as the railroads and Chartiers Creek. The Norwood Hotel is easy to locate, as is the bridge carrying Washington Avenue over the "B & M Branch" of the Pennsylvania Railroad. The Donaldson home, Recreation, in Greenwood is also easy to spot.

The 1921 Bridgeville High School basketball team included, from left to right, (first row) Harry Saperstein, captain Burkey Jones, and Karl Weise; (second row) Mac McIlvaine, Frank Cummings, coach Lloyd McGowan, Paul Rankin, and Frank Barclay.

Steam locomotives hauling hopper cars filled with coal were common sights in Bridgeville in the 1920s on both railroads. Frequently when coal trains stopped to fill the water tanks in their tenders, children would climb onto the cars and throw out coal to be used by their families in heating their homes.

St. Agatha's Roman Catholic Church was organized in 1894 in a small building at 207 Washington Avenue. By 1900, the first church was constructed on Station Street, the site of the present Holy Child Parish facility. The present sanctuary was built in 1931. St. Agatha's parish and St. Anthony's parish were combined in the 1990s to form Holy Child Parish.

The local drugstore was a combination of pharmacy and soda fountain. Bennett's Drugstore, in the Bridgeville Trust Company building, was an excellent example. The drugstores provided home delivery, especially in times of emergency.

The first class to graduate from Bridgeville High School after the new building was constructed on Gregg Avenue was the class of 1926. These students are shown as freshmen in 1923 in front of Washington School.

This early-1920s photograph shows a group of Bridgeville coal miners at the Melrose Mine. Edmund R. Weise (fifth from left, second row) managed this mine. His son Louis is at the extreme right of the second row. Also identified are Martin Gruden (second from left, second row) and John Styche (fifth from left, first row).

Built in Wichita, Kansas, the *Laird Swallow* was America's first commercial aircraft. This photograph shows the extended Mayer family at Mayer Field when the *Swallow* landed there. C. P. Mayer is at the extreme right. The young boy is his grandson, "Buzz" Mayer, standing in front of his father, Charles Mayer. The third man from the right is Elwood "Pop" Cleveland, a well-known barnstormer and, at the time, manager of Mayer Field.

In the 1924 Olympic Games, Bridgeville was represented proudly by Frank Burkhart "Burkey" Jones on the U.S. Soccer Team. Jones is the second person from the left in the second row. In later years, he was a prominent businessman in the community, operating a hardware store and then a service station. He also served as president of the Bridgeville Savings and Loan Association.

The Ernstein Meat Market on Station Street is shown in this 1924 photograph. The men identified in the picture are, from left to right, Mike Gerlach, Ted Lewis, and Tony (last name unknown). The availability of home delivery made it easy for housewives to do their shopping by telephone.

This 1925 photograph shows the five sons of Joseph and Elizabeth Hofrichter in Beadling. They are, from left to right, Albert, Frank, Joseph, Thomas, and Lawrence. The Hofrichters came to the Bridgeville area from the Austrian-Hungarian Empire in 1889. Hofrichter was a coal miner and entrepreneur. In 1924, he established the Limestone Products Company. It is still in operation and managed by members of the family.

Weise House 1200 Bank St.
mid 1920's

The Edmund Robert Weise family built this residence at 1200 Bank Street in 1924. It was razed in the 1970s to permit construction of an apartment building. Weise and his wife, Alma Georgi, had nine children: Frank E., Minnie Alma (Stenzel), Louis August, Paul Herman, Clara Hermina (Jones), Elnora (Rankin), Karl Ernest, Ralph Walter, and Marie Hannah (Brown). The Weise homestead was the first house in Bridgeville to have underground electric wiring, custom storm windows, and an integral garage.

J. D. Meise, one of the group that presented the petition for incorporation, and his family lived in this handsome house at 639 Gregg Avenue. It is now owned by Dr. Audrey Guskey and is a local landmark.

The C. P. Mayer Brick Company used a small shifter engine to move railcars onto the Wabash and Pennsylvania Railroads. The company was organized in 1903 and became a major supplier of paving and house brick in Pennsylvania and its neighboring states. Mayer bricks have a distinctive marking and are popular artifacts for brick collectors nationwide.

The Wabash Railroad provided passenger service into Pittsburgh from this station at the Murray Avenue crossing. Because the line ran "up Miller's Run," it was a welcome asset for folks in that area. Freight traffic continued to be very important on the Wabash and on its successors, currently the Norfolk Southern Railway.

Located near St. Agatha's Church in the late 1920s, Crystal Pool was a popular summertime recreation spot for Bridgeville residents. It was built on the ruins of the Fredrick-Elder Brassworks, which was destroyed by fire in 1923. The houses on Hickman Street are in the background of the photograph.

This photograph, taken inside Foster's grocery store in the 1920s, advertises "good things to eat." Featured are Meuller's spaghetti, Weideman jelly, and Heinz ketchup. Another big seller was Ferry's Seeds, a popular product for amateur gardeners. In those days, housewives could order by telephone and have their groceries delivered to their homes.

Viale's Hotel, shown in 1926, was a landmark on Baldwin Street. By the 1920s, Baldwin Street had developed into a major secondary business district with numerous mom-and-pop operations, combining a residence for the family and a shop for the business. Business continued briskly in the evening until the last train from Pittsburgh, "the bummer," pulled into town and discharged its passengers.

An important ethnic community in Bridgeville was composed of 16 families who emigrated from Syria in the early 1900s, many of them from the small village of B'soma. One of them, the George Corey family, posed for this family portrait in 1927. They are, from left to right, (first row) Marge and Johnny; (second row) Alex, Kay, Mary, and Betty; (third row) Frank, Art, and George.

This photograph shows four handsome young men dressed up for an evening out on the town. They are, from left to right, (seated) Guido Paroline and Ed Salamony; (standing) Pete Cherry and Nino Dalzuffo. All four were longtime residents of Bridgeville and major contributors to the community.

On May 8, 1927, an honor roll was dedicated in front of Washington School, honoring the men and women from Bridgeville who had served their country in World War I. Although the heading of the honor roll clearly states "Boys," there is a section titled "Girls" in the body of the monument.

The Degrosky family was typical of the Lithuanian Americans who lived in Bridgeville. Many families came to this area in the early 20th century to work in the mining and metal industries. Simon and Mary Bilisky came in 1907 from the village of Balbieriskis, near Vilnius, Lithuania. This photograph records the wedding of their daughter Veronica and Charles Degrosky at St. Anthony's Roman Catholic Church in 1927. Also identified in the picture are Eva Aliscky Susa (second from left) and Ann Bakunas Roman (fifth from the left).

Anthony Pesavento was in his hometown of St. Pietro d ValdAstico in Northern Italy in 1920 when his brother Valentino sent money for their brother Guiseppi to come to America. Guiseppi, who had been wounded in World War I, turned down the opportunity; 14-year-old Anthony came in his place. After working as a coal miner and for the C. P. Mayer Brick Company and Universal Cyclops Steel, he apprenticed as a plasterer and eventually started his own plastering business. On October 19, 1927, he married Helen Delach. In the 1950s, he developed a residential community on Cook School Road and Pesavento Drive, naming two streets for his daughters Alice and Nancy.

C. P. Mayer was the dealer for Ryan Aircraft, San Diego, California. The Ryan B-1 Brougham was a sister ship to Lindbergh's *Spirit of St. Louis*. Following his famous transatlantic flight, Colonel Lindbergh made a transcontinental tour of the United States, landing at Mayer Field when he visited Pittsburgh.

This photograph is an aerial view of Mayer Field in the late 1920s, looking northeast. Mayer's house is along the highway, adjacent to the field. Universal Cyclops Steel is visible in the distance. The airport had three cinder runways, the longest being 1,625 feet long.

The Bridgeville All Board Raceway was a world-class facility in the 1920s and early 1930s, hosting many national automobile races. It was located across Chartiers Creek from the Church Street neighborhood of Bridgeville. Bethany Church can be identified in the middle of the photograph. One of Scott's Ponds is in the lower right corner.

Ezio Bigi acquired rights to a bus route from Bridgeville to Dormont Junction (the end of two trolley lines) in 1922. Following his death in 1937, his widow, Mary, continued to operate Bigi Bus Lines. By 1950, Bigi ran 32 round-trips per day between Bridgeville and Pittsburgh, with some routes going as far south as Mayview and Hill Station. This photograph shows driver Lou Bonardi with his Bigi Bus.

One of C. P. Mayer's favorite planes was this Waco biplane. His dress and demeanor in this photograph were appropriate for the Roaring Twenties years.

DEC. 21, 1929 BRIDGEVILLE, PA.
ON MAIN LINE R/W 130' EAST OF BRIDGE 9-A

This 1929 view of the area north of Bridgeville along the Pennsylvania Railroad tracks includes a baseball diamond, the Bridgeville Coal Mine tipple, and Cook's Hill in the background.

In this 1929 photograph, Sam Barzan and Angelo Phillips appear to be taking a break from building a house at 215 Greenwood Place to enjoy a legal beverage. The well dressed gentleman in the photograph is unidentified, although he looks as if he too would feel at home wearing C. P. Mayer Lumber coveralls.

Sam Barzan & Angelo Phillips

1929 - Building house at 215 Greenwood Place, Bridgeville.

Bridgeville School Band - 1930

Bridgeville Band - 1930

Front row: Sam Carson, Alice Weise, Betty Oelschlager, Betty Donaldson, John McCoy, Mario Capozzoli, Marie Dice, Bill Liggett, Russell Simpson, (?).
Second Row: Bill Sullivan, Jane Patton, Ruth Godwin, Betty Bingham, Louyis Asti, (?), Pete Vissat, George Carson, Philip Sportolari, Bob Stuckert, Helen Oelschager, Helen Hassebaugh, (?), (?), George Rittenhouse, Mr. Mercer, director.
Third row: D.M. Bennett, school director, E.O. Liggett, school superintendent, Harry Ziegler, Elmer Beardshall, Roman Bianchin, Ferdinand Demsher, (?), Martha Levi, Kerr Bingham, (?), Frank Rittenhouse, Joe Styche, John Howe, (?), Anna Mary Dondaldson, (?), (?), (?), Robert Wray, high school principal.

Bridgeville High School was always proud of its band. This version, pictured in 1930, is in front of Lincoln High School. The school was constructed on Gregg Avenue and opened in 1925.

The 1930 football team included Vic Vidoni, who later played for Duquesne University and the Pittsburgh Steelers (then known as the Pittsburgh Pirates). Vidoni is believed to be the fifth player from the right in the third row.

Seven

THE DEPRESSION YEARS
1931–1940

Although many Bridgeville families were inconvenienced by the economic turmoil associated with the Great Depression, the community in general was able to cope with its difficulties and maintain an acceptable standard of living.

This was an era of excellent service via home delivery. Housewives could discuss their requirements by telephone with the grocery and the meat market and feel confident that the delivery truck would soon arrive with exactly what they ordered. Other regular visitors were the iceman, the milkman, the bread delivery man, and the fruit and vegetable huckster.

Equally satisfying was the knowledge that any one of a number of highly competent doctors could be summoned to one's home when needed. Many times the doctor's visit was followed by a visit from the quarantine officer and the promise of several days off from school.

Most families had an automobile that was used infrequently for shopping trips and occasional joy rides. The town was small enough that even young children could easily walk to school and come home for lunch. All the children had bicycles that were used continuously. It is hard to believe today that a child could ride his bike downtown in the early evening, leave it unattended while he went to a movie, and then find it in perfect shape when he returned.

Families living in Bridgeville during the Depression years lacked the expensive appliances and luxuries that they enjoyed a generation later, but the overall atmosphere of good service and congeniality more than made up for any deficiencies. Children's sports were not organized by adults, but the kids managed to hang baskets on telephone poles and to level off vacant lots when they needed a place to play.

A wooden trestle carried Mayview Road over Cow Hollow, near Godwin's Nursery. Mayview Road was a major artery linking the state hospital at Mayview with Bridgeville and Pittsburgh. Cow Hollow is a deep gulley cut by a small tributary of Chartiers Creek.

On July 28, 1928, the trestle collapsed under the weight of a steam shovel being driven across it. The driver was pinned under the shovel. Doctors Rittenhouse and Sigmann amputated his leg to permit him to be extracted from the wreckage. He unfortunately died shortly thereafter at Mayview Hospital. The trestle was replaced by an earthen fill and a reinforced concrete culvert that local children called "The Indian Tunnel."

This 1931 family gathering at 624 Chestnut Street includes, from left to right, Margaret Crawford Erhard holding "Fritz," Joseph Warren Thomas, Jean Thomas, Beth Crawford, C. C. "Buzz" Erhard Jr., Joseph Warren Thomas Jr., and Jean Crawford Thomas.

Washington Avenue is seen in this 1930s photograph with a band marching north on it. Two Boy Scouts are walking toward the viewer in front of Butler's Grocery Store. A sign, "Pitt Soda Grill," advertises another establishment farther down the street.

A 19th century wrought iron through truss bridge carried Chartiers Street over the Pennsylvania Railroad tracks. It was replaced by a modern deck girder bridge in the 1990s. A Bridgeville tradition was the courteous way motorists took turns in both directions using the one-lane bridge.

This aerial view of Bridgeville's Lower End probably dates to the early 1930s. Angelo Pepe's Bridgeville Hotel is prominent in the center of the photograph. The bridge carrying Washington Avenue over Chartiers Creek is of classic pony truss construction, with two independent trusses and no cross bracing. By this time, many homes had been built on St. Clair Street and Prestley Road, and the neighborhood had acquired the unique personality that has survived until today.

July 4, 1934

Chartiers Creek has cut down to the level of the Pittsburgh Coal Seam in the Bridgeville area, making strip mining very effective. The residue of such mining in the early 1900s is a series of strip-mine ponds that were recreational sites for local residents. This photograph shows the Gastgeb family enjoying Scott's Ponds, which were south of Bridgeville. The Blue Ponds, halfway between Bridgeville and Mayview; "Elsie's," east of the Washington Pike; and "C. P.'s Ponds" near Presto were also quite popular.

Community Day at Kennywood Park was a popular annual event. These five ladies had their picture taken at the photographer's booth there in 1934. They were, from left to right, (seated) Mrs. Joyce, Mrs. Charles C. Erhard, and Mrs. Bill Bailey; (standing) Mrs. Victor Skelly and Erma Lutz. Mr. Erhard's comment, "In the good old days when a pearly smile was all that was necessary" and his signature "an old flame" appears to be aimed at the two ladies who were not smiling.

The Amoco service station on Washington Avenue was typical of those in the 1930s. The coal tipple for the Bridgeville Mine can be seen at the far left of the photograph and a smoking pile of slack coal directly behind the station.

Bridgeville housewives were always skilled at cooking and making preserves. In this 1930s photograph, Anna Schmidt is shown making apple butter in an outdoor kitchen in the Lower End with help from Carl and Paul.

The Universal Cyclops Steel office building at 311 Station Street was the headquarters for Bridgeville's largest employer in the mid-1930s. In addition to the hundreds of steel workers in the mill, the company employed a large staff of white-collar workers in this building.

By 1935, Neil Brown had come to Bridgeville and had become the Bridgeville High School football coach. He is at the extreme left in the third row. His teams had outstanding success in the late 1930s and early 1940s. Second from the left in the second row is John Wight; he coached the high school teams in the mid-1940s and became principal of the high school in 1950.

This lovely winter scene along Chartiers Creek shows the bridge carrying the Washington Pike over the creek at the north end of Bridgeville. This bridge was constructed in the 1920s to replace an old wrought iron through truss bridge; the bridge at the south end of town was replaced at the same time.

The importance of the railroad to the community of Bridgeville is highlighted in this photograph, taken from the bridge carrying Washington Avenue over the B&M (Bridgeville and McDonald) Branch. Prominent in the picture are the water tower, the siding into Lutz's Lumber Yard, the crossing-guard shack, and the passenger station. By the 1930s, there were 18 trains each way passing through Bridgeville en route to Pittsburgh.

Like every other proud Bridgeville father, Herbert McCormick took lots of pictures of his young son Marvin. Also shown in the photograph are Marvin's mother, Sarah (left); his half sister, Mae Belle; and his half brother, Perry.

The George Baird family lived in this impressive residence at the corner of Chess and Station Streets. The house has been well maintained and is a local landmark today.

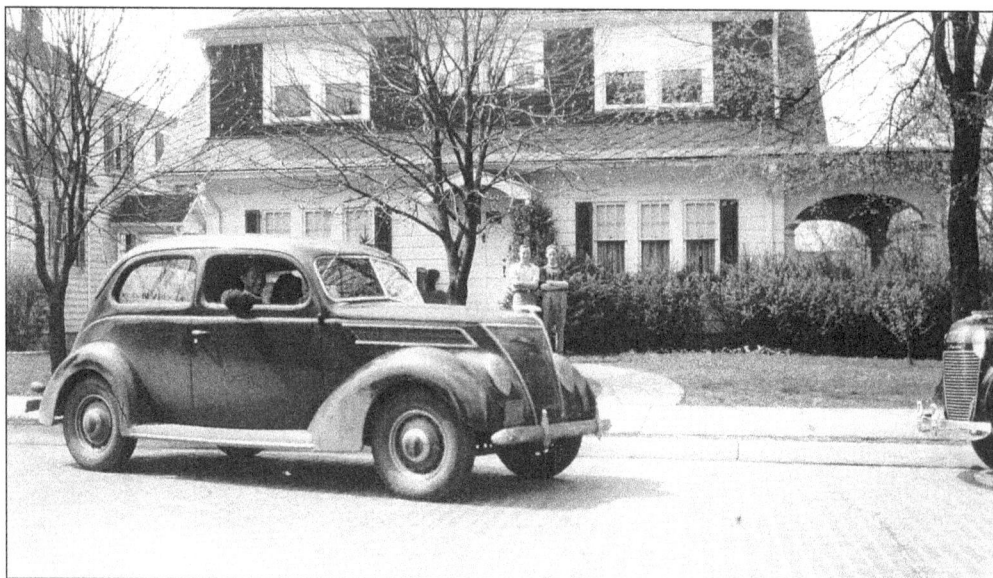

Dr. George Rittenhouse and his family lived at 624 Chestnut Street. He and his wife, Jane Erhard Rittenhouse, are shown in front of their home in their brand new 1937 Ford. Dean Fullerton (left) and Buzz Erhard (right) are standing in the front yard.

Brothers Albert, Gilbert, and Arthur Colussy operated Colussy Motor Company on Baldwin Street. The business was founded by their father, Louis Colussy, in 1918. It is still in existence, at a different site, and is proud of being the oldest continuous Chevrolet agency in the world. Louis Colussy initially was involved with his brothers Peter and Michael in Colussy Brothers Builders, responsible for the development of much of Baldwin Street.

Murray Toney came to Bridgeville from B'Soma, Syria, in 1910 when he was 30 years old. He made his living peddling yard goods throughout the local mining towns between Bridgeville and Washington, Pennsylvania. He saved enough money to send for his wife, Saphia; his son, Samuel; and his daughter, Selma, to join him. They later had two more children, Thomas and Michael. In 1930, he opened a dry goods store on Baldwin Street known as M. Toney and Sons. Marge and John Corey are shown in this photograph across the street from Toney's store and residence.

When Toney's first wife died, he returned to Syria and brought back a new bride, Nassima. Shown here with Toney are his wife, Nassima; his son, Donald; and his daughter, Arlene. Another daughter, Geraldine, was born after this photograph was taken. The Toney family was an example of the ingredients that went into Bridgeville's melting pot.

Toney's business prospered; by 1935, he was able to purchase a brand new Buick. Don Toney is shown with the car in this 1937 photograph. Toney was the patriarch of the Bridgeville Syrian American community when he died at the age of 110 in 1990. He was one of the founders of the St. George Orthodox Church in Bridgeville and the original founder and sponsor of the St. George Cemetery, located south of Bridgeville along the Washington Pike.

Brothers Ernest, Alfred, and Elmer Colussy operated a Ford agency in Bridgeville for many years, complementing their brothers' Chevrolet agency. This 1939 photograph illustrates the triumphal tour of Ford's 27 millionth car. During World War II, their slogan was, "There's a Ford in your future, but the Ford in your past, is the Ford that you've got, so you'd better make it last!" The 1939 Ford was the subject of that slogan. The agency was located at the corner of Washington Avenue and Hickman Street.

By the late 1930s, the Piper J-3 Cub was the most popular aircraft at Mayer Field. Nicknamed "Mayer Crates" by the local children, these planes could be seen in the sky over Bridgeville almost continuously on summer weekends.

In 1939, a new post office building was constructed on the southwest corner of the intersection of Hickman Street and Washington Avenue. The foundation for the new building is shown in this photograph. Dr. Fife's house is in the left part of the photograph; the house behind the foundation was occupied by the Angelo Pepe family.

The new post office was a symbol of the optimism in 1939, as the war in Europe began to generate enough business in the United States to finally make it possible to see the end of the Depression, now 10 years old.

In 1941, as part of the WPA program to encourage the arts, muralist Walter Canelli painted an impressive mural on the front wall of the Bridgeville Post Office. A black-and-white image of it is shown in this photograph. Titled *Smelting*, the mural depicts steelworkers at the Vanadium Corporation.

The Owls Club, located on Baldwin Street, was chartered by the Independent Order of Odd Fellows in 1903. The membership eventually decided to operate independently as the Reliable Fraternal Association, better known as the Owls Club. This photograph shows a soccer team representing the club. Pictured are, from left to right, (seated) Steve Kovach, Zelindo Cimarolli, Frank Zinger, Bud Williams, and unidentified; (standing) ? Oelschlager, Nino Dalzuffo, Omero Cimarolli, ? Bombassaro, Tom Smart, Whitey Miskofski, Blackie Dalzuffo, and Ed Oelschlager.

Bridgeville's Turtle Hunters were a group of men who harvested turtles from Chartiers Creek in the 1930s and 1940s. Their method of hunting was to wade in the creek and reach under the roots of sycamore trees along the shore until they found a turtle. They included, among others, Arthur Maioli (far left, second row), Joe Betschart (third from left, second row), Russell Jones (far left, first row), and Walter Gerlach.

On March 26, 1937, a TWA flight, the *Sun Racer*, crashed near Clifton, killing the pilot, copilot, stewardess, and 10 passengers. To Bridgeville residents, this tragedy brought home the perils of life in the new world in which they were living.

The Women's Club, on Dewey Avenue, provided Bridgeville ladies with a social and cultural outlet in the 1930s. This photograph shows seven of the ladies with a lovely doll collection. The ladies include, from left to right, (seated) unidentified and Toni Giuliani; (standing) two unidentified, May Thomas, Alice Snyder, and Carrie Weise.

Eight

WORLD WAR II
1941–1950

The 1940s brought World War II to Bridgeville; hundreds of its young men and women found themselves far from home. To help them remember their hometown, Jane Patton imagined a night downtown in an article for the newsletter Bethany Church sent to service men and women:

"August 1944: Have you ever dreamed about strolling up Washington Avenue in the evening and tried to just imagine who and what you would see? Saturday night about 8:00 o'clock is the most active time in the old town these days. First we see the Presbyterian Church and manse—the glow of the setting sun behind them gives one a feeling of beauty and serenity.
Grant Pearl is sitting on the front steps at Dr. Fife's. Sam Fryer is going up the street, probably to discuss baseball with some of the boys. Dr. George Rittenhouse is going into his office, which is filled with people. Dr. and Mrs. McGarvey are sitting on the front porch watching our little world go by.

"Holding up the front of Weise's store, stand Ralph himself, Knobby Sam, and Izzy Miller (that is probably the crowd Sam Fryer will join). *Shine On Harvest Moon* is on at the movies, and Mr. Rankin is taking tickets.

"On the bridge sit Malarkey, Delphus, Donelli, and Maruzewski trying to decide what to do with the rest of the evening. On the other side of the bridge there are about thirty people waiting for the Blue Ridge Bus. In the lumber office Mr. Lutz is still working at his desk with that green eyeshade on his head. Pete Strasser is talking to a customer.

"The police car is parked on the corner ready for action. Chief Myers (not in uniform), Artie Chivers (who is on duty), and acting mayor Butch Goldbach are in huddled conversation. There goes Bill Bennett in his car—he must be delivering a telegram; Bennett's is still the Western Union Center. Mr. Foster is trying to pick out a couple of ripe cantaloupes for a customer.

"There are a lot of people in Squire Croft's office—from all appearances it could be either a wedding or a trial. Women now stand guard at the railroad crossing on Station Street. Hudge Villani, driving the Bigi Bus, just rounded the Railroad Street corner."

This eloquent description of downtown Bridgeville is as nostalgic today as it was during World War II.

Dial telephone service came to Bridgeville in 1943, ending the era of telephone operators. James H. Rankin is shown dialing the first call. He was owner and operator of a men's clothing store and two movie theaters. The Rankin Theater, at 527 Washington Avenue, presented three first-run feature films each week. The Strand, on Station Street, ran Class B films, two double features per week, plus serials and the popular "Bank Night."

Weise's News Stand, at 528 Washington Avenue, was a popular destination for any trip downtown. The store was originally owned by the Goehring family; Ralph and Louis Weise purchased it in 1931. After Louis's untimely death, Ralph Weise managed the store with the able assistance of Angelo and Teresa Pennetti.

Ado "Buff" Donelli was the most successful of a large group of successful Bridgeville athletes. Shown playing for the Morgan Strassers in a National Cup soccer game at the Polo Grounds in New York City in 1943, he had an equally impressive career as a football player and coach. He is the only person ever to coach a Division I college team (Duquesne University) and an NFL team (the Pittsburgh Steelers) concurrently.

Bridgeville young men paid a heavy price during World War II. Alex Asti, who is pictured, died when the warship *Juneau* was sunk at Guadalcanal. Also losing their lives were Samuel Allender, Harold Armstrong, Louis Baldini, Robert Bogdewiecz, Wayne Carson, John Fabeck, John Ferris, John Howard, Joseph Kasprzak, Raymond Kramer, Arthur Langer, James McCracken, Edmund Mekolat, Matthew Milk, Regis Moore, John Moutz, Steve Pawlick, Robert Randolph, William Ridder, Karl Schmidhamer, Ronald Simpson, Elmer Straka, and Jacob Yapel.

Bridgeville was represented in the City-County League in 1945 by this baseball team. They are, from left to right, (seated) "Herky" Kerensky, "Mussy" Godwin, Bill Batch, John Barfauldi, A. Pardini, Jim Delphus, Don Babish, and Earl Dawkins; (standing) coach Bill Vosel, coach Pat Malarkey, Bob Hines, Jocko Schneider, Babe Ramous, Bill Alisesky, Nick Mamula, Don Vosel, and manager/sponsor Anthony "Mojo" Vosel. Batboy Jimmy Wagner is in the front.

Weise's News Stand, in addition to its popular soda fountain, boasted an impressive selection of newspapers and magazines. It was an excellent place for the selective shopper to spend hours browsing before deciding whether to buy the latest copy of *Life* magazine or *Newsweek*. Ralph Weise (left) and Angelo Pennetti are shown inspecting the magazine selection in this photograph.

The Thomas Deep family was a prominent part of the Syrian American community in Bridgeville. They came from Somat, Syria, and lived at 643 Baldwin Street. Shown in this 1946 photograph are, from left to right, Donald, Jim, Robert, Joe, Elizabeth (mother), Raymond, Janet, Richard, John, Thomas (father), George, Helen, Ralph, and Ronald.

Shown in front of a 48-star flag are the five Pennetti brothers home safely from World War II. They are, from left to right, Ralph, Angelo, Patrick, Mike, and Jimmy. The Pennetti brothers were five of the many Bridgeville men and women who made up the "Greatest Generation" in the 1940s.

The Bridgeville Indians were a popular drum and bugle corps at parades throughout the area in the late 1940s. Organized by local barber "Skip" Batch, the corps provided an excellent opportunity for young people to perform. Their theme song, "Over There," and distinctive war bonnets announced their arrival at parades and other events. Their majorettes were, from left to right, Dorothy Davis, Francis Cowan, Joan Batch, Esther Pruner, Phyllis Dillenbaugh, Joan Abood, and Emily Sumner.

Many Bridgeville residents are proud alumni of the Bridgeville Indians drum and bugle corps. This 1947 photograph includes, from left to right, (first row) Dorothy Davis, June Heinman, Phyllis Dillenbaugh, Francis Cowan, Esther Pruner, Joan Batch, Joan Abood, and Emily Sumner; (second from left); (second row) Helen Konovich, Shirley Quarture, Sidney Gardner, Gerald Barnes, Alice Spotti, Ella Spotti, Margaret Maurer, Joan Mason, Jay Heiman, Dolores Barnes, Bill Siget, Janet Forno, and Florence Mille; (third row) Norma Davis, Laverne Piconi, Valerie Orbick, Gloria Miller, Margaret Fonti, Ruth Miller, Skip Batch, Sally Fonti, Jim Batch, Bill Batch, Richard Barnes, and Edward Boyd.

The F. Marion Oyler family came to Bridgeville in 1934. Oyler was a civil engineer working for the Pennsylvania Railroad; he was transferred from Dunkirk, New York, to Pittsburgh. The availability of commuter trains to the city made Bridgeville an attractive place to live. With their three-year-old son John in the rumble seat, they drove their Model A Ford to Bridgeville, spent two nights at the Norwood Hotel, then moved into this stone bungalow at 823 Bank Street. It was rented from Silhol Realty; John Capozzoli was the landlord.

In 1937, the Oylers purchased this new house at 1053 Lafayette Street. Their son Joseph was born at the time they were moving. The house and lot were bought for $5,700, a significant investment in the Depression years. The new houses that were built in that neighborhood represented a positive reaction to the difficulties of the decade. They are shown in front of their house in this 1946 photograph.

Boy Scout Troop 245 prospered in the mid-1940s under the leadership of charismatic scoutmaster Eddie Croft. Shown in this photograph are members of the Owl Patrol, from left to right, (kneeling) Philip Walsh at a District Campout at Raccoon Creek Park; (standing) Ed Weise, Bob Harris, Amos Jones, Don Brown, and Don Heller.

After Eddie Croft left Bridgeville, Dick Hobson became scoutmaster; Troop 245 continued to provide an excellent opportunity for young boys with a love of the outdoors. This photograph shows a group of scouts hiking along Morrow Road. From left to right, they are Larry Davis, Paul Love, Dale DeBlander, Eddie Macdonald, Dennis Neuman, and Bob Maioli.

Shown after a snowstorm in the late 1940s, Gloria Sam's Ice Cream Store on Baldwin Street was typical of the many small businesses that flourished there. A walk down Baldwin Street provided a diverse shopping experience.

In 1948, Bridgeville High School won its second WPIAL (Western Pennsylvania Interscholastic Athletic League) Class B football championship. The 1942 team, coached by Kass Kovalcheck, had defeated Leetsdale 12-0 for the first championship. The 1948 team was undefeated in the regular season and defeated Marion High School 24-0 in the championship game. In the third row of this picture, head coach Bob Hast is at the extreme left, and assistant coach Clyde "Tiny" Carson is at the right.

The Albert and Sadie Sam family gathered for a portrait in the late 1940s. They are, from left to right, (seated) Katharine, Gloria, Sadie (mother), and Norman; (standing) Thelma, Ann, George, Kenneth, Marion, and Edna.

The coronation of the May Queen each spring was a major event at Bridgeville High School. In 1949, the queen was Sally Russell, shown here with her attendants Jeanne Squarcha (left) and Marian Jones (right). The 1948 May Queen, Louise Duchess, is at the far right of this photograph. She passed her crown on to the new queen.

Representing the Veterans of Foreign Wars, these proud veterans of World War II participated in the 1948 Memorial Day parade. They are shown on Washington Avenue just as the parade passed the Rankin Theater and the Central Restaurant. The Memorial Day parade has been a Bridgeville tradition for many years, usually terminating in a service at Melrose Cemetery.

This photograph of the 1948 Memorial Day parade is taken farther down Washington Avenue. Signs for Cappelli's Restaurant, Sapersteins Clothing Store, and Pepe's Bar and Grill are prominent.

Memorial Day 1948 provided an opportunity for the dedication of an honor roll for veterans of World War II. It was located along Railroad Street between American Legion Post 54 and the Universal Cyclops Building. The Legion Hall is at the right side of the photograph. The majorettes from Skip Batch's drum and bugle corps, the Bridgeville Indians, are at the left corner of the building. This honor roll and the World War I honor roll shown on page 79 were replaced by an honor roll at 430 Washington Avenue that commemorated all Bridgeville service men and women.

Washington St., Business Section, Bridgeville, Pa.

This photograph shows a busy Bridgeville business district in the late 1940s. The photograph is looking north on Washington Avenue from a point south of its intersection with Station Street.

112

The Bern-Hart Motor Company represented
Chrysler Corporation for the sale of Dodge
and Plymouth automobiles in this facility
on Washington Avenue in 1950.

Although the Norwood Hotel's function as a
resort hotel became less significant, it continued
to provide Bridgeville with hotel, restaurant,
and bar and grill services for many years. This
photograph shows the hotel as it looked in 1950.

Like all the other ethnic groups in Bridgeville, the African American community was a major part of the "Greatest Generation" during World War II. Their service helped provide a foundation for the civil rights movement after the war. Typical of the Bridgeville servicemen was Henry Perkins, shown in this photograph. Following his service in the war, he was one of the founders of the Randolph-Simpson American Legion Post, named in honor of Robert Randolph and Ronald Simpson, two Bridgeville African Americans who lost their lives in the war.

Founded in 1903, the First Baptist Church has been the religious and cultural center of the Bridgeville African American community for over a century. In this photograph, Herbert McCormick is shown receiving an award from Curtis Copeland in recognition of his service to the church. Both men were active in the Bridgeville Civic League, founded in 1951 "to provide a program of cooperation and race relations among the people." Copeland also served as postmaster at the Bridgeville Post Office.

Bridgeville resident Bill Winstein, shown here at his desk at the *Pittsburgh Press*, was an outstanding sports cartoonist, known for the photographic-like realism of his drawings. Bridgeville athletes were among his favorite subjects.

A Bill Winstein sketch honored three members of the Bridgeville High School 1949 football team: Lou Cimarolli, Ken Beadling, and Anthony Capozzoli. This team was the third Bridgeville High School squad to win a Class B title in the 1940s by defeating Trafford High School 64-0.

BOB O'NEIL

Defensive end . . . has played offensive guard
. . . a versatile athlete . . . a "team" player
. . . only American to play on French Rugby
team while he was in military service.

Bob "Huck" O'Neil was a valuable member of the 1948 Class B WPIAL (Western Pennsylvania Interscholastic Athletic League) championship football team. He later played college football at Duquesne and Notre Dame and professional football for the Pittsburgh Steelers and the Calgary Stampeders. He is shown here in a Steeler publicity photograph.

Abramovitz's Food Store, on the corner of Baldwin Street and McLaughlin Run Road, was another successful small business in the Baldwin Street neighborhood in the late 1940s.

Nine

TRANSITION
1951–2001

The economic, social, and cultural changes that occurred in the United States in the second half of the 20th century were not as drastic as in other times, but their impact on small towns in southwestern Pennsylvania was dramatic. Bridgeville was affected significantly.

A community that had relied upon manufacturing facilities for much of its employment was hurt when manufacturing declined. Some industries relocated their plants to areas with cheaper labor and, eventually, overseas. The children of mill workers were forced to find alternative employment in the service industries and in white-collar jobs.

The advent of broad ownership of automobiles and inexpensive gasoline led to the development of shopping centers surrounded by free parking lots in neighboring townships. Mayer Field was replaced by the Great Southern Shopping Center. Many businesses relocated to the shopping malls. Small operations, especially the neighborhood mom-and-pop stores, struggled to stay in business.

The two movie theaters ultimately closed, unable to meet the competition from television and from the multiscreen theaters in the malls. The easy access into downtown Pittsburgh, by bus and by private automobile, provided additional competition to the local businessmen. Passenger service on the railroads succumbed to competition from buses and automobiles. Both bus lines were acquired by the Port Authority Transit in a county-wide consolidation of transportation. The resulting service was effective but lacked the personal touch of its predecessors.

Unfortunately, the hope that World War II was indeed "the war to end all wars" was soon crushed. James Huey, Edward Kolessar, Robert Shipe, Harry Stringer, and Amos Jones lost their lives during the Korean War. Richard Johnson, Leslie Sam Patton, and John Schardong died while in the service during the cold war. The Vietnam War claimed Kenneth Brown, James McAleer, and George Verdinek.

Consolidation of the Bridgeville School District with Collier Township, Scott Township, and Heidelberg into the Chartiers Valley School District spelled the end to public schools in Bridgeville. New schools were built remote from the community, and the experience of walking to school was replaced with bussing. No longer was the high school the center of culture for the community.

A group of progressive citizens organized a youth baseball program in 1951. This evolved into the more formal Bridgeville Athletic Association, which was chartered and incorporated in 1957. In 1975, girls' softball was added to the association.

The Golden Jubilee Parade in 1951 celebrated the community's 50th birthday. It is shown as it progressed down Baldwin Street. The Colussy Motor Company and Asti's Sport Shop are prominent along the street. Beyond Asti's is the home of the Pickerene family, an unidentified house, then the house occupied by the Fagan family, and finally the home of the Corey family, which included Corey's Poolroom. The porch on the left side of the street is at the home of the Delphus family.

Celebrating 75 years in the funeral home business, the Samuel B. Fryer Funeral Home was represented in the Golden Jubilee Parade by this 19th-century horse-drawn hearse. The Fryer family has continued in this business from 1875 to the present. This photograph was taken on Railroad Street, in front of McMillen's Drugstore.

Teenage boys delivered daily and Sunday papers—the *Pittsburgh Press*, the *Pittsburgh Sun Telegraph*, and the *Pittsburgh Post Gazette*. This photograph shows the 1951 Christmas party Ralph Weise sponsored for these young people. They are, from left to right, (first row) Anthony Dourlain, Ron Beltrame, Sam Minney, unidentified, Tom Zirwas, and Bill Ross; (second row) Bob Barclay, David Cooper, Angelo Pennetti, Ralph Weise, Santa Claus, a *Post-Gazette* representative, Larry Tonarelli, and Jim McCaffrey; (third row) George Fiorintini, Frank Martincic, Jerry Spinnenweber, Jan Yenchick, Joe Oyler, Bob Daly, Gene Kruluts, Steve Nagle, Brent Bradburn, Ron Caruso, D. Kline, and Dale Hilty; (fourth row) Bill Fein, Tom Sells, Jerry Martincic, W. Colley, unidentified, Tom Munnell, unidentified, and Ed Sells.

The Italian Club continued to prosper. This photograph of its officers in the early 1950s includes, from left to right, (seated) Angelol Pedrotti, Herman Orlandini, Anthony Pesavento, Valentino Pesavento, Arthur Beltrame, and Rudy Beltrame; (standing) Settimo Mondine, Eugene Cagliari, Angelo Minella, Jim Vaglia, John Pesavento, Christy Mazza, Elio Dreon, and John Gill.

The Bridgeville Taxi Company did a booming business in the early 1950s from its stand on Station Street. The Jones-Lyne Auto Agency and the Norwood Hotel are in the background of this photograph. As private ownership of automobiles increased, the demand for public taxi service decreased to the point where it was no longer a viable business.

Larry Donovan was a prisoner of war for 40 months during the Korean War. His Lower End friends greeted him in a homecoming party at Lou Kaufman's Bar in October 1953. Pictured are, from left to right, (first row) Bill Hanley, Dan Zampini, James Boyce, Bill Donovan, James Donovan, Ray Donovan, Larry Donovan, and Bill McCaffrey; (second row) Tony Cancelmi, Jimmy Boyce, Bert Quinn, Chuck Degrosky, Steve Smelko, Joe Zampini, Bob Critchlow, Chuck McCaffrey, Art Harter, and Ed Ritenour.

The establishment of the Bridgeville Public Library, the acquisition of the old Pennsylvania Railroad Station, and the conversion of the station into an effective library facility combined to create one of the most positive happenings in the community in the latter half of the 20th century. The founders of the library association were Louise Crump Bergstrom, Grace McDivitt, Betty Mihalyi, Betty Mincemoyer, Betty Sutton, and Sylvia Saperstein.

The civic-minded citizens involved with the establishment of the Bridgeville Public Library acquired a scrapped railroad caboose, renovated it to serve as a children's library, and moved it onto a short section of track adjacent to the library. Ernie Mihalyi was the driving force behind renovation of the library and the caboose. The library was dedicated in 1970; the caboose in 1975.

The resulting combination of the restored station and the attached caboose provided an effective space for the library, as well as a very attractive artifact of days gone by for the community.

The area west of the railroad in front of the Bridgeville Public Library was converted into Triangle Park, featuring trees, shrubs, pedestrian benches, and a handsome gazebo. It has become a popular spot for folks interested in relaxing in a pleasant urban setting. The gazebo has become a popular spot for celebrations.

An excellent example of the effort made to restore downtown buildings to their original appearance is the northeast corner of the main intersection in Bridgeville, Washington Avenue and Station Street. This photograph shows the building as modernized by Union Bank.

This photograph illustrates the results of the restoration of the building in the photograph at the top of this page, returning its appearance to that of the 1930s.

The Norwood Hotel was destroyed by a fire on March 15, 1961. The only remaining artifact of this wonderful old institution is this wrought iron fence post that was lovingly restored by Ted and Diane Evangelista at the Evangelista Hair Care Center at 514 Dewey Avenue. The center is on the eastern edge of the former grounds of the hotel.

When Universal Cyclops Steel moved its corporate headquarters out of Bridgeville, the Greater Pittsburgh Guild for the Blind acquired the building and opened its new rehabilitation facility at 311 Station Street in 1968. Dedicated to helping adults with vision disabilities achieve independent living, the guild served thousands of clients. Bridgeville residents supported their efforts as volunteers and as employees.

This photograph of Washington Avenue in the late 1990s illustrates the Main Street characteristic of Bridgeville, an old-time feel that has survived into the present, with trees, street lamps, and attractive storefronts.

The visit of a restored Pennsylvania Railroad locomotive to Bridgeville and its photograph in front of the Bridgeville Public Library was a nostalgic reminder of life years earlier.

EPILOGUE

At the beginning of the 21st century, there are many reasons for Bridgeville to be optimistic about the future. The community survived many social and economic changes in the second half of the 20th century; in many cases the transitional processes provided strengths that will serve well in the future.

The desire that many people have to return to the order and comfort of the traditional American hometown has produced a trend in which new communities are being designed to mimic the feel and appearance of the kind of town Bridgeville was in 1950. Neighboring South Fayette Township has planned a new town center on the site of the Selden chemical plant, complete with a synthetic downtown.

A recent study of the "walkability" of communities, based on an arbitrary system evaluating access to necessary services and discretionary attractions, gave Bridgeville a rating of 82, far higher than its four neighboring townships whose average rating was 27. Although the quantitative significance of such a study is questionable, it does reflect qualitatively the advantages of living in an old-fashioned small town with a well-defined business district and the Main Street feel.

Bridgeville is blessed with an intact infrastructure—well ordered streets and alleys, paved sidewalks, and neighborhoods—that is delineated by geography rather than by the whims of a developer. It is still possible to walk to the churches, the post office, social clubs, stores, and the library.

The decline in manufacturing jobs has produced a diversity that is immune to the problems of a community dependent upon a single major employer. No longer can a strike or layoff at Universal or the Vanadium have dire consequences for the entire town.

The plans for the new public library and the transfer of its present facility (the rehabilitated Pennsylvania Railroad station and caboose) to the historical society are examples of the progressive personality of the community's leadership.

Today Bridgeville is part of Greater Pittsburgh with easy access to the cultural assets of the city: professional major league sports teams; the Pittsburgh Symphony, Opera, and Ballet; world-class museums; and outstanding universities. Two nearby interchanges for I-79 open up the entire interstate system to the motorist; the nearby Pittsburgh International Airport is a gateway to the entire world.

The people who grew up in Bridgeville half a century ago are grateful for the environment and experience of their youth. It seems probable that this situation will continue well into the future.

Visit us at
arcadiapublishing.com

www.ingramcontent.com/pod-product-compliance
Lightning Source LLC
Chambersburg PA
CBHW080602110426
42813CB00006B/1385